All about the Boston Harbor Islands

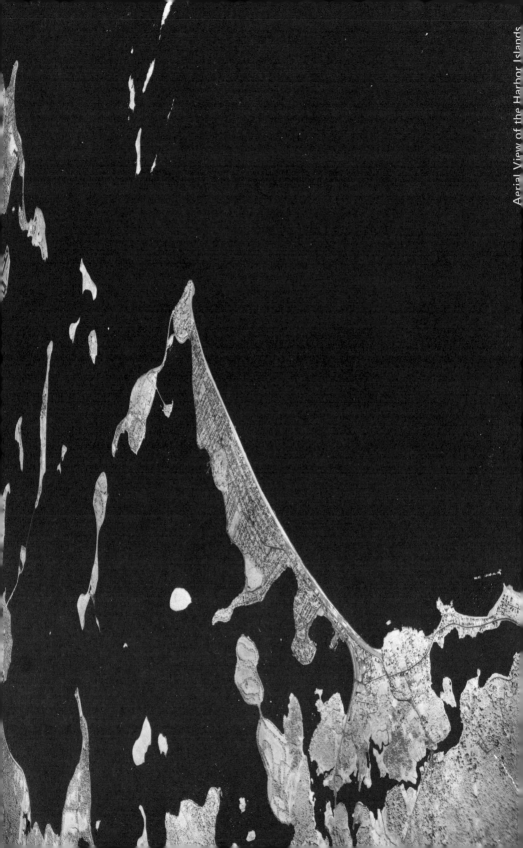

All about the

Boston Harbor Islands

Fourth and Revised Edition

by Emily and David Kales

Maps and sketches by Deborah Warren

Hewitts Cove Publishing Co., Inc.

Hingham Shipyard, 349 Lincoln Street

Hingham, MA 02043

Library of Congress Catalog Card Number: 75-24955

Paper ISBN 0-9636000-0-1

First Edition published 1976. Fourth Printing 1980. Revised Edition 1983.

Revised Edition 1993.

Printed in U.S.A.

ACKNOWLEDGEMENTS

We wish to acknowledge the following works, which proved invaluable in the research and preparation of this book:

Boston Harbor Islands Comprehensive Plan, by the Metropolitan Area Planning Council.

The Islands of Boston Harbor (1630-1971), by Edward Rowe Snow.

History and Master Plan: George's Island and Fort Warren, by Shurcliff & Merill.

Archaeological Investigations at Fort Independence on Castle Island in Boston Harbor, by William A. Turnbaugh.

King's Handbook of Boston Harbor, by M. F. Sweetser.

The Fourth and Revised Edition was revised and edited by Katherine Donegan with the invaluable assistance of the following people:

Marsha Bach, Spectacle Island Park Advisory Committee; Al Kenney, Department of Environmental Management; Barbara Luedtke, Department of Anthropology, University of Massachusetts, Boston Campus; Gary McCann, Muhheconneuk Inter Tribal Committee; David McCarron, Massachusetts Division of Marine Fisheries; Suzanne Gall Marsh, Friends of the Boston Harbor Islands; Sheila McGann, Massachusetts Water Resources Authority; and Michael Neelon, Commercial Photographer.

—Emily and David Kales

The Revised Edition was edited by Nancy Witting.

The Friends' logo was designed by Lynne George.

The Fourth and Revised Edition was revised and edited by Katherine Donegan with the invaluable assistance of the following people:

Marsha Bach, Spectacle Island Park Advisory Committee; Al Kenney, Department of Environmental Management; Barbara Luedtke, Department of Anthropology, University of Massachusetts, Boston Campus; Gary McCann, Muhheconneuk Inter Tribal Committee; David McCarron, Massachusetts Division of Marine Fisheries; Suzanne Gall Marsh, Friends of the Boston Harbor Islands; Sheila McGann, Massachusetts Water Resources Authority; and Michael Neelon, Commercial Photographer.

Join Friends of the Boston Harbor Islands, Inc.

The FRIENDS, founded in 1979, encourage public use of the islands balanced with the need to protect this fragile ecosystem and historic environment. This non-profit, environmental-education organization has a three-fold mission: advocacy, direct service, and public education. It sponsors year-round activities including: boat trips, on-island volunteer programs, community events, and the Boston Harbor Islands Revegetation Project.

The FRIENDS evolved out of the efforts of the Boston Harbor Islands Volunteer Corps. The Corps was organized in 1979 by Suzanne Gall Marsh to supplement the program services of the Boston Harbor Islands State Park.

The FRIENDS administer the On-Island Volunteer Program for the various agencies involved in the management of the Park. These volunteers assist the Park staff by giving island tours, providing Park information to the visitors, and doing trail work and special projects. Their ages range from 18 to 80. Families, along with their children, are welcome to participate. All volunteers receive orientation/training and free boat transportation when working on the islands.

FRIENDS' members range from newcomers to the Boston area to those who remember the islands before they become a state park. All members share a concern for, and an appreciation of, the islands. The FRIENDS are the core group for this unique recreational resource located so near a major metropolitan area.

All who wish to learn more about the islands, to care for them through volunteer service, or to support the FRIENDS are invited to join us as members. Our constituency is truly grass-roots. We give direct service and are a visible presence, whether on a remote island or at a Beacon Hill public hearing.

Membership Benefits

- an informative newsletter,
- reduced rates on FRIENDS trips and on the public ferries to the Islands,
- merchandise and publications discounts,
- volunteer-training programs,
- social events and special outings, and
- the peace of mind and satisfaction which comes with doing one's part for the environment which we all share.

For information about Friends of the Boston Harbor Islands, Inc. send a self-addressed stamped envelope to Post Office Box 9025, Boston, MA 02114. You can contact them at 523-8386. The FRIENDS maintain a South Shore branch office in the Hingham Shipyard, 349 Lincoln Street, Building 45, Hingham, MA 02043; telephone 740-4290.

FRIENDS BOSTON HARBOR ISLANDS

TABLE OF CONTENTS

I INTRODUCTORY

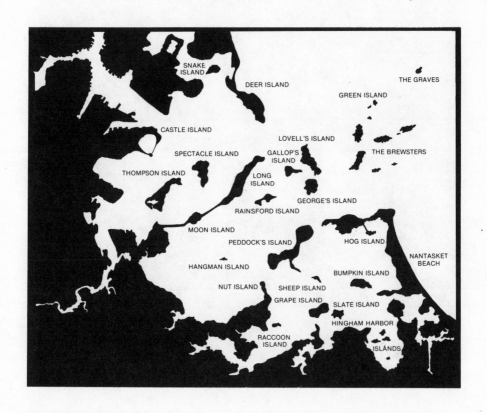

Boston Light, the First Lighthouse in America,
Erected in 1716 and Rebuilt after the Revolution

THE PROMISE OF BOSTON HARBOR

Man has always been fascinated by islands. They stir the imagination with dreams of adventure and romance, of Paul Gaugin and Robinson Crusoe. Yet while the local armchair traveler is longing for some faraway exotic paradise, he might be, completely unaware that right at his own front door lie the islands of Boston Harbor—for the most part under-utilized and "undiscovered." Yet these islands lie within a 25-mile radius of more than 3 million metropolitan Boston residents.

Boston Harbor, an area of some fifty square miles, is bounded by 180 miles of shoreline and dotted with some thirty islands which together cover about twelve hundred acres of land. Through the years, neglect and misuse have taken their toll. Pollution, antiquated institutions and military activities have diminished the opportunity for the public to enjoy these little-known but superb natural resources. With the commercial growth of the postwar years, several islands have even been obliterated; the former Governor's, Bird and Apple islands have become part of the extended runway system of Logan International Airport.

Fortunately, almost all the Harbor Islands are now publicly owned, protected from further abuse and damage. Several state agencies as well as the City of Boston are working not only to protect the islands for conservation, but to develop them for recreational and educational pur-poses as well. While it will take some time to fully protect the islands'

Mystic River Bridge—Inner Harbor

ecosystems and develop their recreational facilities, the visitor will discover much to enjoy right now.

Besides the physical beauty of many of the islands—some of it lush, some quite stark—perhaps most striking is the contrast they offer between dynamism and tranquillity. From his island vantage point, the visitor can watch the bustle and drive of a modern metropolis—planes roaring over Logan, oil tankers gliding through the channel, cranes hauling cargo from freighters, the expanding skyline of financial Boston towering in the distance. But then he can turn away and, meandering up a deserted, overgrown trail, disappear into the solitude of an island grove.

A journey to the islands offers a diversity of experiences, not all of them pleasant, but nonetheless reflecting accurately the surrounding world. The thoughtful observer will be able to see in these islands a microcosm of the problems urban man has wrought: dumps, water pollution, debris in the Harbor. He will see both the fragility and hardiness of natural resources on the islands and sense the challenge to restore them to their former beauty and charm.

Large Commercial Ships Still Make Frequent Trips to Boston

FROM THE BEGINNING

Eons ago the crust of the earth shifted. Earthquakes were set off, volcanoes erupted, and titanic floods were unleashed. As the earth shook and rocked, a block of its crust broke off and sank, forming a lowland plain—the Boston Basin. Millions of years passed and then the glaciers moved down from the north, grinding down ridges of land and leaving smooth, narrow hills of glacial till called drumlins. (The two most famous examples of these formations are Beacon Hill and Bunker Hill.) As the glaciers melted, the sea rose in the basin and surrounded many of the drumlins. These drumlins became some of the islands of Boston Harbor.

Legend says that the first white man to set eyes on what is now Boston Harbor was the Norseman Leif Ericson in A.D. 1003. Perhaps John and Sebastian Cabot, English explorers sailing down the North American coast in the fifteenth century, were the first to spot it. Historical records suggest, though, that it was either Bartholomew Gosnold, an English voyager to this part of North America in 1602, or a Frenchman, the Sieur De Monts, in 1604, who first discovered the Harbor.

In any event, the first white man to settle in the area was the Reverend William Blaxton, an Anglican clergyman who in 1625 took up residence on what is now Beacon Hill. This one-man settlement became a community when the Massachusetts Bay Company, a group of Puritans headed by John Winthrop, landed on "Blaxton's Peninsula" in 1630. Shortly afterward, they renamed the settlement Boston.

THE ARRIVAL OF GOVERNOR WINTHROP'S FLEET IN BOSTON HARBOR, 1530.
[AFTER THE PAINTING BY W. F. HALSALL.]

From that time on, Boston flourished as a great port. By 1660 virtually all imports from the mother country to New England passed through Boston Harbor. By the middle of the nineteenth century Boston had become a top-ranking international port, and Donald McKay's clipper ships, built in East Boston shipyards, plied the seas from Canton to Cairo. While the Harbor has deteriorated in the twentieth century, containerization and other developments in shipping are now helping to restore Boston Harbor to commercial prominence.

Even before the white man arrived, the Indians were making use of the natural resources of the Harbor Islands, raising crops on them and fishing off their shores. The English settlers cut down the trees on many of the islands to clear land for grazing cattle and sheep, to farm, and to provide wood for shipbuilding and firewood for nearby towns and settlements.

Several of the islands were used for other purposes in early times. On Thompson Island, a trading post was established where Indians traded beaver furs for articles brought by European voyagers. Deer Island was renowned among hunters, since deer often swam out to the island, seeking refuge from wolves on the mainland. From Slate Island, slate was hauled off to build homes for Boston's thriving citizens.

In the eighteenth century, the Boston Harbor Islands became a popular resort area. Excursionists from the mainland flocked out to inns and guesthouses on the Brewsters and Long and Peddock's islands to imbibe the salty air and indulge in the illicit pleasures of gambling and watching boxing matches. In many cases, the fresh produce from the island farms was served in inns and hotels.

CLIFFS ON THE OUTER BREWSTER, AT LOW TIDE.

When a wave of social reform washed over Boston in the nineteenth century, the islands furnished a convenient place to establish hospitals, reformatories, poorhouses and prisons. In fact, one of the most famous Union prisons for Confederate soldiers during the Civil War was established at Fort Warren on George's Island.

Throughout the last three centuries, the Harbor Islands' greatest role has been in local and national military defense. Settlers were originally attracted to Boston by its large, well-protected harbor, islands, peninsulas and hills which offered easily defensible locations for communities around the harbor.

The islands and hills also played a strategic role during the Revolutionary War. The British occupied Boston and its Neck, but failed to occupy the nearby hills. George Washington's troops occupied Dorchester Heights (now part of South Boston), a promontory overlooking the harbor. With the Continental Army holding a commanding military position, the British fleet was threatened in the harbor, while their troops were effectively besieged in Boston. On March 17, 1776, the British, realizing further resistance was futile, evacuated Boston for good.

The Harbor Islands continued to provide a coastal defense in the nineteenth century. During the War of 1812, Fort Independence on Castle Island helped to spare Boston the British amphibious assaults that befell such other ports along the Atlantic seaboard as Baltimore. And no doubt, the addition of Fort Warren on George's Island as well as other island fortifications in the Civil War deterred any Confederate raider from making an attack on the port city.

Fort Warren in 1898: Defense of Boston Harbor

With the outbreak of World War I, the predominant use of the islands once again was for defense. During World War II, nine islands in the Harbor were fortified and the entrance to the harbor was heavily mined and fenced off by an underwater torpedo net. Radar-controlled coastal batteries, which could hit an enemy ship thirty miles away, were set up, and antiaircraft batteries, along with those at Portsmouth, New Hampshire, and Providence, Rhode Island, could blanket the skies above the entire Massachusetts coast.

After the war, the period of neglect began. Guns were dismantled, fortifications were abandoned, and the remaining installations became overgrown with thick brush and weeds. Docks and piers decayed and deteriorated, their rotting wood adding to the harbor's flotsam. Once the site of some of the country's most progressive hospitals and prisons, the islands became graveyards for outmoded institutions and desolate repositories for society's unwanted—human beings as well as human wastes. Abandoned and neglected, indeed almost forgotten in the last twenty-five years, the islands lie dormant, waiting to be discovered once again.

The Harbor is composed of several distinct geographical areas: the Inner Harbor, the Outer Harbor (the Brewsters), Dorchester Bay, Quincy Bay and Hingham Bay. This guidebook is organized according to the geographical locations of the islands in the Harbor. It is our hope that it will help the island visitor interpret this unique environment by guiding him through the past and into the future, showing him where we have been and where we are going.

Rowe's Wharf, the Boston Harbor Hotel, and the Commuter Boat Terminal

Boston Skyline

Docking at Commercial Wharf

U.S.S. *Constitution*—"Old Ironsides"

Commercial Motif

Dedicated to Edward Rowe Snow (1902-1982)

A Day's Catch Arrives at Boston Fish Pier

Newly Restored Faneuil Hall Marketplace, Looking Towards Harbor

Faneuil Hall (lower right)

Now a contemporary urban commercial center, the Marketplace consists of three long market buildings built in 1826 by Mayor Josiah Quincy from the design of architect Alexander Parris. The center building, the Quincy Market, reopened August 26, 1976 on its 150th birthday, features a variety of eating places, food stores and food-related specialty shops. The flanking South and North Market buildings have distinctive retail shops on lower levels and offices on upper.

III   THE ISLANDS OF DORCHESTER BAY

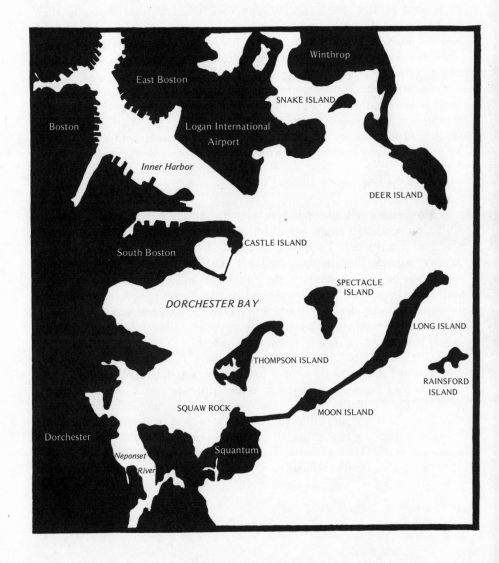

CASTLE ISLAND

Overlooking Boston Harbor from the hill atop Castle Island, watching huge jets from Logan Airport crisscross against the sky and cargo ships being unloaded at the nearby Massport terminal, one feels the thrust and dynamism of a modern metropolis all about him. What a sudden contrast, then, to turn around and pass through the massive granite walls of Fort Independence to enter a world of long ago. For not only is Castle Island—linked to South Boston since 1891—the most accessible of the Harbor Islands, but its major role in early American history makes it an essential point of interest for any visitor to the Boston area.

Fort Independence, the venerable grandfather of the Harbor's forts, is recognized as the oldest continuously used military fortification in the United States. Its antecedents go back to 1634, when the Puritan governor and his advisers sailed over to Castle Island one day, ascended its steep cliffs, and decided it was by far the best defensive site in the Harbor for the new colony.

Each man in the scouting party contributed the lordly sum of five pounds, and before long the first "fort"—composed of two wooden platforms supporting a small mud house—was erected on the island. The crushed-oystershell masonry of this structure—labeled "a castle with mud walls" by one of its early commanders—soon crumbled, and it was replaced by a larger fort of pine wood and stone. This in turn fell into ruin from fire and the passing years, and so another fort, even sturdier and more elaborate, was constructed.

When Samuel Sewall, that stern old Puritan judge who presided over the Salem witchcraft trials, rowed out to Castle Island in 1701 to observe this new construction, he was so shocked at the earthy language of the military engineer that he cautioned the workmen to obey the engineer's orders but be deaf to his imprecations. Our Puritan forefathers also objected to the noise of musketry practice which wafted over the Harbor to compete with the marathon sermons of such preachers as Cotton Mather. As a result, they passed a law prohibiting the soldiers on Castle Island from shooting their guns on the Sabbath.

As the drama leading to the Revolutionary War unfolded, however, Castle Island began to take on a particularly significant role. More and more the fort became a refuge for British officials and Tories who were arousing the ire of the Boston citizenry. There was ample precedent for this: back in 1689 Sir Edmund Andros was held prisoner at the fort because he had the misfortune to be appointed the colony's governor by King James II. The colonists denounced the despotic James in favor of the more democratic William of Orange, who challenged and overthrew him in England's "Glorious Revolution." Some fifty years later, as Bostonians were moving irrevocably toward their own revolution, it was noted that "an uneasiness took hold in Boston" and another unpopular governor "evacuated to the Castle" (as the island's fort was known) until things simmered down.

So when the Stamp Act was enacted by Parliament in 1765, one of the first in a series of hated taxes levied on newspapers, deeds, and legal documents, it seemed only natural that the nervous Governor Bernard should store the controversial stamps under guard at the Castle. Nor was it surprising that when Lieutenant Governor Hutchinson took command of the Castle and spent thousands of pounds to repair the fort's 210 guns, few Bostonians were anxious to help him. Given the history of the island as a Royalist refuge, they could well have reckoned that those guns would some day be turned on them.

Such speculation soon proved to be true. Tension mounted in the streets of Boston between British soldiers quartered in the city and colonists, culminating in a riot one wintry night in March 1770, when a harassed group of Redcoats fired into the mob, killing five men. To prevent any further incidents such as the "Boston Massacre," the British regiments were packed off to Castle Island, which became Royalist headquarters from that point on.

In the wake of the Boston Tea Party, followed by the fateful events at Lexington and Concord, the island's guns were indeed turned on Boston patriots. The British commander of the Castle attempted to lead his regiment toward Salem to confiscate gunpowder and military supplies, but he was forced back to Castle Island by alert local militiamen who detained his troops at the ferries. In another futile mission, the Redcoats set out from Castle Island to attack American posts in Roxbury, but only succeeded in burning five houses in Dorchester. Finally, the British command set out with five hundred men, hoping to outflank Washington's batteries

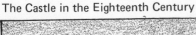

The Castle in the Eighteenth Century

on Dorchester Heights. But a fierce storm combined with blinding fog blew the Redcoats way off course, allowing Washington to maintain his advantageous position. Even though the guns on Castle Island hammered away at Dorchester Heights, Washington's Continental Army had the enemy surrounded, and the British gave up and prepared to pull out of Boston at last.

The British didn't go quietly, however. Before taking leave of their Castle Island headquarters, they loaded mines and set the island on fire. Here is a contemporary account by a British officer of the Royal Engineers of the demolition operation:

> March 20, 1776 . . . found the Rebels had begun a new work on Dorchester Point opposite Castle William. We fired at them from the Castle. . . . About two we observed about 21 whale boats set out from Dorchester Neck and row across to Thompson's Island, where they landed a small cannon and pull'd it to the point and fired on our working Partys on Spectacle Island. At 3 o'clock Colonel Leslie came to the Castle from the General with orders to load the mines. . . . The Barracks and other houses were then set on fire and at 9 the Rear Guard consisting of 3 Companies, the Artillery, etc., Embarked and we got all safe on board the Transports.

After dumping the fort's remaining ammunition in the Harbor, the Redcoats sailed out of Boston, blowing up Boston Light as they passed through the Outer Harbor.

Civil War Troops at Fort Independence

General George Washington wasted little time in restoring the fort on Castle Island. Master craftsman Paul Revere was dispatched to replace the shattered cannons, and each man in Boston was required to donate one day of service restoring the fort's batteries. By 1779 John Hancock was named commander of a "new" Castle; he was replaced several years later by fellow Revolutionary hero Sam Adams. And in a ceremony in August 1799, President John Adams renamed the Castle "Fort Independence," in honor of the newly created United States of America.

Although Fort Independence was manned during the War of 1812 (when the British, hearing of its formidable defenses, decided to stay away) and served as a military camp during the Civil War, it was never again to see action. A major catastrophe did take place there, however, during the Spanish-American War, when the U.S. Government was using Castle Island as a mine and torpedo station. Some mines were in the process of being unloaded when a powderhouse exploded, leaving four men dead and blowing a great hole in the seawall surrounding the island.

Over the years, Castle Island was the site of both the first state prison and New England's first marine hospital, as well as an important observation post in both world wars. But nothing went quite so far to spread its fame as the arrival in 1827 of an obscure young man who enlisted in Battery H of the First Artillery under the assumed name of Edgar A. Perry. Later known to the world as Edgar Allan Poe, this eighteen-year-old

Fort Independence Today

Bostonian was even then attracted to the macabre, and during his five months there he learned of the fort's most grisly incident.

It seems that back on Christmas Day 1817, two officers fought a duel because one had accused the other of cheating at cards the previous night. A young lieutenant, Robert Massie, was killed in the duel and his friends decided to avenge his death. They got Massie's killer drunk and then led him to a small chamber deep in one of the fort's lowest dungeons. After shackling him to the floor, they sealed up the entrance and left the man to die. The tale would appear to have been confirmed in 1905, when some workmen renovating the fort knocked down a wall and discovered a skeleton, still dressed in the remnants of an old military uniform. At any rate, Poe based his famous short story "The Cask of Amontillado" on the episode—although he changed the setting from Castle Island to the catacombs of a European nobleman.

These days, more remains of the past are being dug up at Castle Island, and while they may not be as startling as a ghoulish skeleton, they are significant in themselves. Since early spring of 1974 an archaeological team has been searching for artifacts buried in the parade ground and interior rooms of Fort Independence. To date this team has turned up over five thousand objects, some of them dating as far back as 1740. Together, they form a fascinating picture of the life of eighteenth- and nineteenth-century soldiers.

We know what they ate from oyster and clam shells, pig and chicken bones; what they wore, from buttons of uniforms and jewelry; and how they fought, from grapeshot and cannonballs that have been dug up at the fort. The artifacts also tell us how the soldiers whiled away the time—frag-

Aftermath of Explosion during Spanish-American War

ments of a domino face, a glass marble, and more than one whiskey bottle have been discovered. The remains of chamberpots and bone toothbrushes, silver candle snuffers, and Wedgwood plates also give a good picture of household equipment of bygone eras. Interesting, too, are the sites of these archaeological digs, some of which the MDC, which manages the fort, plans to put on public display along with many of the artifacts uncovered.

The MDC has restored Fort Independence, which—like so many of the island fortifications—had fallen into ruin over the years. The curious visitor may have a look at some of the areas that have already been cleaned out, such as the officers' quarters, or the magazine, where black powder was stored in special spaces to keep dry. Old fireplaces, latrines, and cisterns are of interest, as are the heavy doors with dates and initials carved in them. The amateur archaeologist might even stumble across some artifact—like a Civil War era musketball.

Facilities: The area surrounding Fort Independence has long been a popular recreational spot for Bostonians and includes facilities for picnicking, a concession stand, a fishing pier, comfort stations, a tot playground, and walks offering wonderful cityscape views. On Pleasure Bay nearby, there are swimming beaches and sailing lessons through the MetroParks Harry McDonough Sailing Program from late May through early October.

Since 1975, Fort Independence has undergone major construction work. The reconstruction of the Pleasure Bay causeway and the seawall has been completed, and Fort Independence is open again for scheduled tours. The Castle Island Association hosts periodic tours of the fort for the general public. You can write to the Association at Box 342, South Boston, MA 02127. For more information, contact the MDC Harbor Region at 727-5290.

How to Get There: By auto—From Boston take the Southeast Expressway (I93). Get off at South Boston-Dorchester, exit 17. Turn left onto Columbia Road and continue on to a rotary. Turn right halfway around rotary onto Day Blvd. and follow shoreline to fort. By public transportation—MBTA, take City Point or Bayview Bus from Broadway, Copley Square or Dudley Station.

SPECTACLE ISLAND

Over the years, the 97 acres of Spectacle Island have received more than their share of abuse. Lying between Castle and Long islands, Spectacle was originally formed by two drumlins connected by a low sandbar. The island's name is presumably derived from its former resemblance to a pair of eyeglasses. But over the centuries, erosion and landfill have radically altered its shape, and now one would be hard put to guess the origin of its name.

Historical records indicate that in colonial times, when Spectacle was used for agriculture and fine timber, pastures covered the slopes of the island's hills. In 1717, a quarantine hospital was established on the island. Many ships, such as those which came from Ireland in 1729 carrying smallpox, were required to discharge passengers and crew at Spectacle. The hospital operated for twenty years and then moved to Rainsford Island.

In the nineteenth century, Spectacle became a popular spot for Sunday boating excursions and picnics. Two resort hotels were opened in 1847 and for ten years carrried on gambling activities until a police raid closed down the games. Shortly afterward the hotels went out of business.

After the hotels closed, Nahum Ward purchased the island and set up a rendering plant. Slaughterhouse offal and nearly two thousand horses a year were rendered into hides, glues, horsehair and neat's-foot oil. Thirty employees, several of whom lived on the island with their families, worked at the rendering factory. The island provided a convenient place for the City of Boston to dispose of dead horses that otherwise would have presented a serious health hazard. In the early 1900's, though, demand for Ward's products declined along with the supply of dead horses as the automobile and electric trolley began to replace carriage and wagon. By 1910, the rendering plant was out of business.

In 1921, the City of Boston signed a contract with a private company to reclaim grease from the city's garbage. The garbage was brought to

Remains of Grease Extraction Plant on Spectacle

Spectacle and cooked and compressed to extract grease, which was then sold to a soap manufacturer. The processed garbage was dumped on the island and covered over with rubbish. In the 1930's, the market for reclaimed grease declined and the grease plant went out of business. The ruins of the grease extraction plant, in particular a 90-foot draft chimney, still stand today as the dominant man-made feature and symbol of the island's use—or more aptly, misuse.

The City continued to dump raw garbage and rubbish there until 1959, when the South Bay Incinerator in Boston was opened. Throughout the years, this dumping actually increased the size of Spectacle by 36 acres and the piles of garbage are estimated to be over 100 feet deep.

The final ecological insult to Spectacle was its use as a repository for a salvage firm. The unsightly debris remained on Spectacle and leached heavy metals into the Harbor. Changing tides brought rusted metal, broken glass and other trash to neighboring coastal areas.

Legislative leaders recognized this significant source of harbor pollution and enacted laws directing cleanup of the island and its conversion to a public park. Appropriations for the plan were negotiated over a ten year period as part of the Central Artery/Third Harbor Tunnel Project. Environmental groups lobbied governmental agencies and are now involved in the planning and design of the park through the Spectacle Island Park Advisory Committee (SIPAC).

Excavated fill from the Artery project will provide the cap to the island. Stabilization of the shoreline will be achieved through construction of a stone sea wall and dike. The planting of trees, shrubs, flowers, and grasses to stabilize the topsoil will also provide a habitat for wildlife.

The significant contribution of SIPAC in the areas of architectural and environmental design is reflected in the current park plan. The public may expect to enjoy a public marina and pier, visitor center, amphitheater, wading beaches, and trails when the park opens in 1997.

THOMPSON ISLAND

If Spectacle Island is the ugly duckling of the Harbor Islands, then Thompson (or Thompson's) Island, its neighbor in Dorchester Bay, is the heralded beauty. Lying just off the Squantum section of Quincy, Thompson consists of 157 acres, some 50 acres of which are salt marsh. Trees, wild flowers and open fields cover the entire island. On the northeastern end is a fine beach. The northwestern side is mostly rocky. A long sandbar extends from the southern portion, nearly connecting the island with Squantum at low tide.

The island was first settled by David Thompson, who established a trading post with the Neponset Indians in 1626. The island was acquired by the community of Dorchester in 1634 and for over two and a half centuries was leased to several different families for farming.

In 1883, The Boston Asylum of Indigent Boys moved to the island. Two years later, the asylum merged with the Boston Farm School Society and the name was changed to the Boston Farm and Trade School. The institution provided both a home and school for boys who were deprived of an adequate home life.

By the late nineteenth century, the school had developed an excellent farm with a herd of cows, pigs, horses, turkeys, hens and some beef cattle. Much of the marshland was drained and diked for pasture. Vocational training and farming continued until the middle of the twentieth century.

But the increasing emphasis on a college education led to a change in the school's curriculum, and the poor economic circumstances of the farm led to its discontinuance. Both farm and herd of cows were phased out and a more traditional academic curriculum was instituted. In 1955, the school was renamed Thompson Academy, reflecting the shift in educational emphasis. In 1975 the focus was again shifted to reflect changing times. The island is now an outdoor learning center for both children and adults.

Most of the academy's existing buildings were constructed in the early twentieth century. A gymnasium and a dormitory are among the newer structures. The athletic fields and buildings are located on rolling upland in the middle of the island. Dirt roads extend from the northern to the southern end of the island, which is mostly lowland.

Salt Marsh on Thompson Island

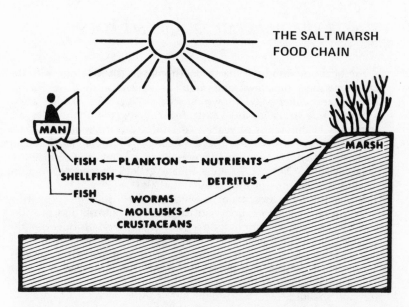

THE SALT MARSH FOOD CHAIN

A considerable portion of this southern area is a tidal pond and salt marsh. Baby fish, clams and a great variety of birds feed in the marsh, which is rich in nutrients. Among the various kinds of fowl are common egrets, killdeers, ring-necked pheasants, green herons, shorebirds and songbirds. The marshes are also feeding and loafing stations for resident and migratory ducks, geese and brant.

Throughout the island are stands of oak, maple, cherry, birch, pine, willow, hickory, elm, horse chestnut and linden and an apple orchard. Open fields from the abandoned farm and wildflowers make it an entomologist's delight. In the late summer the island abounds with butterflies—monarchs, swallowtails, cabbage butterflies and other varieties.

Facilities: The Thompson Island Outward Bound Education Center conducts discovery programs for Boston schoolchildren and meetings for schools, churches, temples, corporations and associations; as well as recreational and special events. It has residence halls for 150, an auditorium, gymnasium, dining and conference areas, environmental study areas, a challenge adventure course, and Interpretative Trail walks. Although located within the Harbor Islands State Park, the Center is an independent non-profit corporation.

How to Get There: Thompson Island is accessible only by commercially licensed passenger vessels and its own vessel, "Pilgrim IV." For information and reservations, call 328-3900.

LIFE AND DEATH OF THE SALT MARSH

The tidal pond and salt marsh on Thompson Island, along with the other marshes, meadows and mudflats which border the Harbor Islands, are collectively known as coastal wetlands. These areas, which include virtually every coastal lowland affected by the tides, are formed over thousands of years as the tides deposit sediment across bays and estuaries along the coast, isolating shallow waters. Gradually these shallows fill in with silt, become mudlfats, and are colonized by tough marsh cordgrasses. As these aquatic grasses die and decompose, they form a detritus of fine organic particles.

This detritus has two major functions. It nourishes the growth of more varied vegetation such as blackgrass and bulrush and provides the base of the estuarine food chain. Distributed throughout the estuaries and coastal waters by the tides, the detritus is consumed by worms, mollusks and crustaceans, which in turn are eaten by fish. Some of the detritus also breaks down into nutrients that are eaten by minute organisms called plankton. Plankton in turn is eaten by finfish and shellfish—which are ultimately consumed by man.

Coastal wetlands provide a buffer zone between the land and sea. In a heavy storm, the danger of flooding is significantly reduced as the salt marshes, acting like a natural catch basin, collect the waters pouring in from the uplands—waters that otherwise would flood the inhabited lowlands. Then slowly the marshes release the waters into the ocean. The wetlands also reduce the danger from tidal floods by absorbing the blows of pounding waves from the sea. It is estimated that without salt marshes the flood damage from one of the furious northeasters that periodically slam into the Massachusetts coast could exceed $10 million.

As a unique and irreplaceable habitat for many species of plant and animal life, the salt marshes provide vital spawning, feeding and nursery grounds for such sport and commercial fish as striped bass, bluefish and winter flounder. Newly hatched bluefish, for example, swim from deep waters into the tidal marshes. Here they mature and, as adults, head back into deeper water. Flounder and striped bass spend much of their time in the shallow waters of the coastal marshes.

The shoal waters of the salt marsh offer an invaluable nesting and winter habitat for many species of shorebirds and waterfowl. Destruction of the marshlands, coupled with the indiscriminate use of pesticides, is directly linked to the decline of many birds such as the marsh hawk, red-shouldered hawk and osprey that use this special habitat.

The fact is that coastal wetlands are the most productive ecosystem in the world. An acre of salt marsh may produce as much as ten tons of organic matter per year—more food than the richest acre of wheat. Such an abundant food supply supports the large inshore populations of pollack, winter flounder and shrimp. In Dorchester Bay alone, nearly $400,000 in revenue generated annually from sport and commercial fishing can be directly attributed to the productivity of the marshlands. If Massachusetts lost all its tidal marshes, commercial fishing along the coast would be seriously damaged as a unique natural environment disappeared.

People—with their penchant for acquiring and discarding—are the major destroyers of coastal wetlands. The result is that these wetlands are filled in to make more room for seashore cottages, shopping plazas or convenient dumps. Bridges, roads, parking lots and marinas built over marshes all have taken their toll too. Even man's slightest touch, such as widening a channel, has been enough to upset the delicate ecological balance of the salt marshes. Today only 1200 acres of salt marsh remain along the shoreline and islands of Boston Harbor —a small percentage of what existed before World War II.

Substantial progress has been made in the battle to save coastal wetlands. In the last decade, the rise of local conservation commissions and the establishment of the Cape Cod National Seashore have greatly helped to preserve some coastal wetlands in Massachusetts. Further aid came when, in 1963, Massachusetts passed the Jones Act (later merged with the Wetlands Protection Act in 1972), which granted the state's Department of Natural Resources the power to regulate any dredging or filling of coastal wetlands that might harm marine life.

In 1965, under the Coastal Wetlands Act, more regulatory control was granted to Natural Resources to protect tidal marshes by restricting their uses. Protecting the tidal marshes, however, is a lengthy process requiring identification and public hearings. Nevertheless, as of the end of 1974, nearly 26,000 acres of coastal wetlands in Massachusetts have been permanently preserved by restricted usage.

Despite this progress, trouble areas still exist. The pressure to develop docks, marinas and other seashore recreational facilities, particularly on Cape Cod, has not diminished. Some careless individuals continue to dump their wastes into the salt marshes. While destruction has slowed considerably, acres of salt marshes in Massachusetts are destroyed yearly.

Ultimately, not laws, but people—all the people—can save wetlands. However, to convince everyone that the wetlands are imperiled is no easy task, for much of the damage to this fragile ecological system goes on unseen. But everyone must become concerned about the value of coastal wetlands. For every time a bulldozer fills in a salt marsh, we irrevocably destroy what nature has taken over five thousand years to build.

DEER ISLAND

Once a "real island," Deer Island was connected to the mainland town of
Winthrop in 1936 by the filling-in of a narrow channel called Shirley Gut. Deer
is a glacially formed island called a drumlin. It overlooks President Roads, the
main shipping channel entering Boston Harbor.

In colonial times, forests covered the island. It apparently derived its name
from the deer that fled from wolves on the mainland by swimming across Shirley
Gut or crossing the ice in the winter.

The advantage of using an isolated, but accessible island in Boston Harbor
for internment and incarceration was first recognized in Colonial times. Two
months after the start of the King Philip's War in 1675, the Puritan government
issued a proclamation directing hundreds of friendly Christian Indians to leave
their villages and relocate to Deer Island. The island's resources were not adequate
to feed them, and no assistance was rendered from the mainland. At least two
hundred perished from starvation and disease during the first two months of
internment. Prisoners of war were also brought to Deer Island and later sold into
slavery.

The memory of these Native Americans is honored each year through a reenactment of the trip from the old Natick village site to Deer Island. The group,
which includes descendants of Deer Island internees, gathers on South Natick
common on October 30 and traces the route taken more than three hundred years
ago. Members of the Native American community have expressed concern that
their ancestral gravesites on Deer Island have been disrupted by the construction
of the Massachusetts Water Resources Authority wastewater treatment plant.

With the construction of a quarantine hospital in 1847, Deer Island again
provided a holding area for the displaced. Almost 5,000 Irish immigrants were
admitted to Deer Island between 1847 and 1849. Many were taken ill during
their long voyage from Ireland. 750 died and were buried on the island.

The House of Industry, Deer Island

In the middle of the nineteenth century, a reformatory was built on Deer Island. This facility was converted into the Suffolk County House of Correction in 1896. The relocation of the House of Correction in 1991 ended Deer Island's history as one of the oldest continuous penal institutions in the United States.

The Harbor Entrance Command Post during the Second World War was located on Deer Island. Fort Dawes was built at the tip of the island by the Army, and the Navy operated a radar and signal station. All remnants of this World War II heritage were recently demolished in order to provide space for the construction of the nation's second largest wastewater treatment plant.

Two million cubic yards of earth were moved in 1991 in order to create the level platform necessary for the construction of the 1.3 billion gallon plant. Ferries transport construction workers daily to Deer Island from Squantum Point and Rowe's Wharf. The new primary treatment plant is scheduled for completion in 1995, and the secondary treatment plant by the year 2000.

Facilities: Contact the M.W.R.A. Office of Public Affairs at (617) 241-6057 if you would like to arrange a tour of the treatment plant on Deer Island. In April of 1994, buildings housing the original steam pump station and the visitor reception are scheduled for completion.

How to Get There: By auto—take Shirley Street in Winthrop. Road crosses the causeway to Deer Island.

THE STONE CUTTERS

Convicts at Work.

HOW THE DEER ISLAND SEWERAGE TREATMENT
PLANT WORKS

The first stop for raw sewage from Greater Boston communities is one of the three headworks on the mainland—at Chelsea, Roxbury and South Boston. Here the sewage passes through screens which remove sizable objects like rags, cans and logs that have found their way into the sewer system. The sewage then goes through a degritting process, removing materials like sand and coffee grounds.

Following screening and grit removal, the sewage travels by gravity flow from the mainland through two deep rock tunnels under Boston Harbor to Deer Island. The tunnels are each about four miles long and eleven feet in diameter.

Nine massive pumps at Deer Island, located six stories below their diesel engines, raise the sewage from the tunnels up to the sewage treatment units. The pumping units are designed to handle maximum flows of nearly one billion gallons daily.

Huge sedimentation tanks on the island separate scum and sludge from the sewage. The settled sludge is pumped into thickening tanks and brought together with recirculated sludge in digestion tanks. In the digestion tanks, sewage sludge is changed from organic material to an inert substance.

New Improvements

- On December 24, 1991, M.W.R.A. locked the valve controlling passage of sludge from the Deer Island Treatment Facility into the harbor. The 400,000 gallons of liquid sludge produced daily are transported to the Fore River Staging Area in Quincy for conversion into fertilizer pellets.
- As of February 1989, the daily release of 10,000 gallons of scum has ceased. Scum is now treated on land.
- The amount of heavy metals and toxic chemicals dumped daily from M.W.R.A. treatment plants into the harbor has decreased.

Deer Island Sewerage Treatment Plant

BOSTON HARBOR'S WATER

Over the years portions of the Harbor, especially the Inner Harbor, have become severely polluted. But in recent years, dramatic improvements in the quality of Harbor's waters have taken place. Visitors to the islands may be interested in current pollution conditions in the Harbor and prospects for further water quality improvement.

Debris is the most visible form of pollution, a hazard to navigation as well as an eyesore. Flotsam and jetsam in the Harbor may come from rotting piers and wharfs, aging buildings along the Boston waterfront, or sunken hulks as much as three hundred years old. Refuse is constantly being dropped into the Harbor by ships and shoreline residents. Just about anything thrown into the Charles, Mystic or Neponset rivers ends up in the Harbor, too. Several programs are now under way to control debris pollution. Among these are island cleanups and removal of dilapidated piers. The U.S. Army Corps of Engineers is also involved, identifying rotten hulks, pinpointing waterfront structures in need of demolition or repair, and keeping the Harbor free of large debris that could endanger navigation.

Sewage is by far the greatest source of pollution in Boston Harbor. Significant progress has been made since 1968, when the MDC put into operation its sewage treatment plant at Deer Island. Previously much of the sewage from 45 communities, with a population of more than 1.5 million, had been dumped—mostly untreated—into the Harbor. It is now pumped through underground tunnels, screened and heavily chlorinated at Deer and Nut islands; then the treated wastewater is released into the sea.

Sewage pollution, however, is still far from being under control. Many communities have antiquated combined storm and sanitary sewer systems which in rainy periods carry raw sewage, along with stormwater runoffs, into the Harbor. During the last few years, combined sewage overflows, which occur when the system's capacity is exceeded, have decreased. Improved treatment of the overflow by the three new treatment facilities has resulted in improved water quality (particularly in waters adjacent to the facilities). The installation of the new pumps at Deer Island and improved maintenance of the sewage infrastructures have been important steps in the right direction. There are still more sewage overflows and sewage contaminated storm drains to be identified and corrected in the years to come.

The harbor is now more aesthetically pleasing due to the reduction of scum and sludge. The swimming beaches have also shown an improvement in water quality over the past two years, and beach closings due to high fecal coliform counts have been reduced. The health of the marine life in the harbor has been monitored by fishermen and scientists. The occurrence of diseases in fish, such as fin-rot and tumors, has declined. Average concentrations of organic chemicals in seafood from Boston Harbor (excluding lobster tomalley) have been measured at less than the regulatory limits. The water quality must still improve and more time for healing must pass before the fish and shellfish in Boston Harbor are as clean and healthy as those in offshore waters.

SOURCE: *The State of Boston Harbor: 1991,* Massachusetts Water Resources Authority, Charlestown, Massachusetts

Long Island Shoreline Where the Water Quality Is Good

IV   THE ISLANDS OF THE OUTER HARBOR: THE BREWSTERS

Facing out toward the vast Atlantic like lonely sentinels, the stark, windswept Brewsters stand farthest to the east in Boston Harbor. The islands include Great Brewster, Little Brewster, Middle Brewster, Calf, Little Calf, Green, Shag Rocks and the Graves.

The formation of the Brewsters dates back in geological time to the ice age. Great Brewster is a drumlin, created by deposits of glacial till and and clay. The other islands of the Outer Harbor are rocky outcroppings, formed as the ice sheet tore away pre-glacial soils and ground down the hills to bedrock. It is believed that millions of years ago, the Brewsters might have been a single land mass. But continuous erosion by the wind and sea eventually separated the huge mass into several smaller islands. At low tide, when the shallow water surrounding the islands recedes to reveal partially submerged boulders and sandbars, it is easy to see how the islands might have originally been connected.

The islands were named for Elder William Brewster, Plymouth's first preacher and teacher, who along with Captain Myles Standish explored the Harbor in 1621. After Brewster died in 1641, the Town of Hull acquired the islands and in the 1680's sold them to private citizens. Today, all the Brewsters are once again in the public domain.

These islands, together with adjacent water, islets, rocks and flats, will be developed into the Boston Outer Harbor Sanctuary. Emphasis will be placed on preserving the wild, marine-dominated environment rather than on providing intensive recreation.

GREAT BREWSTER

The largest of the outer islands, 23-acre Great Brewster is dominated by a large drumlin, 100 feet high. The signs of erosion are clearly etched on its slopes. The island's profile dips into a shallow valley of marshland and continues upward into another, much smaller hill at the southwestern part of the island.

While little is known about early activity on the island, there is evidence that it was farmed in the early nineteenth century. In 1848, the City of Boston bought the island and turned it over to the Federal Government. Congress appropriated funds to construct a Quincy granite seawall around the island to protect against further erosion by fierce sea winds. Part of the seawall still stands today.

The island has long boasted a lighthouse. The Town of Hull erected one on the northern bluff in 1681 that predated Boston Light on Little Brewster. The lighthouse was subsequently demolished, but another navigation aid, Bug Light, was built on spidery stilts as a manned lighthouse in 1856. But Light was rebuilt as an automatic light in 1930. It is located at the end of a long sandspit which extends more than a mile southwest of the island. At high tide the spit is covered; but it is almost possible to walk all the way out to Bug Light at low tide.

At the outbreak of World War I and again in World War II, the Federal Government took possession of the island and built fortifications to protect the entrance to the Harbor. During World War II, a sophisticated bomb- and chemical-proof bunker system was constructed. This command post contained electronic equipment which controlled the operation of the Boston Harbor minefield in conjunction with other facilities on George's and Deer islands. On top of the northern bluffs was a battery of 90mm rapid-fire guns to protect the Harbor against fast-moving torpedo boats. Several observation and searchlight stations were part of the installation, and temporary buildings housed the men required to operate the facility. The remains of these buildings still stand today.

Vegetation on the island is sparse. There are a few trees, but in general plants do not grow as fast as on the more protected inner islands. However, wild roses growing in profusion provide a dazzling display of color in the summer.

Perhaps of all Great Brewster's natural features, the most fascinating are the tidal pools and intertidal zone. The intertidal zone is that part of the beach between high tide and low tide lines. Since it is a drumlin-formed island with long stretches of beach, Great Brewster offers easy access to the surround-ing intertidal zone. In contrast, the island's rocky shoreline in the northwest part is dotted with a number of small tidal pools—micromarine environments created by the ebbing tide leaving behind pockets of water in crevices, grooves and low areas.

Both the intertidal zone and the tidal pools abound in marine life. Here are found periwinkles, blue mussels, barnacles, snails, starfish, crabs, sea anemones and horseshoe crabs, those living fossils whose history goes back 300 million years. For the beachcomber, the intertidal zone and tidal pools are a treasure trove of seashells.

Facilities: Great Brewster has no docking facilities; a pier is available for loading and unloading only. Other facilities include a picnic area, pit toilets, four campsites and trails. The trails offer panoramic views of both the Inner Harbor and Atlantic. Island Managers are in residence from June through Labor Day. There are occasional scheduled day trips. Call the D.E.M. at 740-1605 for more information. No water is available, and all trash must be carried off the island. (Note: As of April, 1992, storm damage to pier has not been repaired.)

How to Get There: Access is by private or chartered boat. Permits are required for group day use and camping; register two weeks in advance. (See additional Park information, page 105.)

MIDDLE BREWSTER

The least accessible of all the Harbor Islands, Middle Brewster is a high, 12-acre rocky outcrop. Several steep cliffs drop precipitously to the ocean. Off its shores are underwater ledges and jagged rocks that jut through the surface at low tide, but lie submerged, a hidden danger, in high water. A thicket of small trees exists on the southeastern side of the island and there is a freshwater marsh, surrounded by brambles and cattails, on the eastern end.

The first recorded inhabitants were a small colony of fishermen who established a settlement on the island in 1840. Fish and lobsters were caught in abundance among the craggy rocks just off shore. In 1871, Augustus Russ, founder of the Boston Yacht Club, purchased the island and built a summer villa there. He then leased several lots to other summer residents.

About the only inhabitants now on the island are the seagulls that nest on the east end of the island and the rats that feed along the shoreline. The only traces of human habitation are stone walls and foundations of old summer homes.

Recently, however, the island's wildlife population has increased as a number of blue night crown herons have returned to establish a rookery in a few trees at the southeast corner. These birds, which are uncommon in the region, had been driven from the island by a fire a few years ago and were nesting principally at Peddock's Island. Because of the need to protect this significant rookery and the fact that access to the island is very difficult, recreational use of Middle Brewster is discouraged.

On the Middle Brewster.

Villa of Augustus Russ, Esq., on the Middle Brewster.

OUTER BREWSTER

Climb one of this island's rocky cliffs and gaze out at endless ocean stretching before you. Then turn about and you'll be rewarded by a rather breathtaking view of Boston's skyline off in the distance. The most easterly of all the Harbor Islands, 17.5-acre Outer Brewster is also the largest outcrop of solid bedrock in the Harbor, its rugged terrain contrasting dramatically with the more protected and placid islands in the Harbor.

Several acres of grass and brush grow on the island, but nary a tree. On the northwestern side of the island, the explorer will discover Pulpit Rock, named for its shape and the sounds made by winds sweeping over its flat top, reverberating like a minister's powerful, mournful sermon.

The island was purchased in 1799 by Nathaniel Austin and remained in the family for many years. One of Austin's sons, Arthur, quarried granite on the island for building purposes. Several roads and buildings still extant in Boston are believed to have been constructed with Outer Brewster granite. According to one report, Austin intended to use the quarry site as a small boat harbor. A cove on the northeast end of the island marks the site of the old quarry and proposed harbor.

In 1941, the Army took over the island and built Battery Jewell, a completely self-sufficient installation. The battery consisted of two 6-inch radar-controlled guns, operated by 125 men. Personnel were housed in three reinforced concrete barracks. The battery itself, which was bomb- and chemical-proof, was built into a man-made hill containing tunnels and ammunition storage rooms. A radar unit, mounted on a 100-foot tower, could direct the fire of the guns with accuracy up to 15 miles. The installation even had its own desalinization plant for fresh water supply. After

Outer Brewster with Calf and Little Calf in the Background

OUTER BREWSTER

Camping Areas

View

Intertidal Zone

Pulpit Rock

Barracks

View

W.W.I Gun Emplacements

Boat Access

the war, the site was deactivated, and the island was sold as surplus property in the early 1950's. The deserted concrete barracks and the Battery Jewell still stand, silent testimony to the island's importance during World War II.

Facilities: Outer Brewster is a sanctuary returning to its natural state. There are no facilities. There is evidence of asbestos in the buildings, and visitors are discouraged.

Great Brewster and Boston Light

LITTLE BREWSTER

This island's chief claim to fame is Boston Light, the oldest lighthouse in North America. As eighteenth-century Boston became a booming port, merchants and shipowners realized the need for a powerful beacon at the Harbor's entrance to guide incoming ships. From the time it was erected in 1716, Boston Light began to play a strategic as well as a navigational role. Throughout the rest of the colonial period, Boston Light would raise the Union Jack flag to signal military authorities at Castle Island of approaching vessels. Castle Island would then alert the city to prepare its defense.

During the Revolutionary War, British and American forces vied for control of Boston Light. In 1775, the Redcoats captured the light and blocked entrance to the Harbor. American troops counterattacked, at first unsuccessfully. Then a Major Tupper, commanding three hundred Continentals dispatched by General George Washington, attacked and put the lighthouse out of commission—but not without suffering heavy casualties. As the Continentals prepared to leave the island, they found their boats were stranded on the outgoing tide. Finally, they got their boats free with the British in hot pursuit. It wasn't until American cannons on Nantasket Head zeroed in on the British craft that the Continentals managed to make it back to Boston.

Boston Light in the Nineteenth Century

Soon after, the British evacuated Boston in March 1776. British marines, smarting from American offensives, blew up Boston Light. But because of its strategic importance, in 1783 the State of Massachusetts rebuilt the light—the very same structure you see today. In 1790, the Federal Government took possession of both Little Brewster and the lighthouse.

The War of 1812 found the British once again in Boston Harbor. Within sight of Little Brewster, the British ship *Shannon* engaged the American frigate *Chesapeake*. The *Shannon* won the battle, but immortality went to the Americans in the end, when wounded Captain James Lawrence of the *Chesapeake* shouted his famous command, "Don't give up the ship!"

Boston Light Today

Today the 98-foot-high granite lighthouse is operated by the U.S. Coast Guard. Accompanied by the blasts of a foghorn, its beacon, flashing at 10-second intervals, shines 16 miles out to sea. Boston Light has been declared a National Historic Landmark, and is currently open to public visits.

CALF ISLAND

Directly north of Great Brewster is Calf Island, a flat 17-acre rock mass covered with weeds and high grasses. Situated in the middle of the island is a shallow freshwater pond surrounded by tidal marshes. The island is deserted except for those hardy tenants, the gulls and rats.

Calf Island was probably named after Robert Calef, a Boston merchant, who wrote a book called *More Wonders of the Invisible World.* The tract apparently helped to dispel the witchcraft hysteria that had gripped New England in the late seventeenth century.

The island is sometimes referred to as "the Home of the Lonely Grave." According to an old account, an unknown ship was wrecked and washed up on the island's shore. The unidentified crew members were buried by fishermen on the island in unmarked graves.

In the nineteenth century, a small colony of lobstermen inhabited the island. Archeological exploration uncovered some items of every day use, such as bits from clay smoking pipes, ivory spines from a fan, and children's toys. These artifacts may have belonged to the colorful patriarch of the group, James Turner. In 1883, the island was the scene of illegal boxing matches.

In 1902, Benjamin P. Cheney and his wife, actress Julia Arthur, purchased the island and built a mansion on a cliff overlooking the southeastern shore. Today, you can see the remains of these ruins of foundations and two stone chimneys, bearing the initials "B.P." (Cheney). The main house and boat house were destroyed by fire after World War II. In 1971, vandals torched the remainder of the estate.

Facilities: Calf Island offers foot trails and the remains of old building sites. There is beach access only to the island. Day use and weekend camping are permitted. Camping permits are required and may be obtained by writing or calling Park Headquarters (See Additional Park Information, page 105). Island Managers are in residence weekends only from June through September. Pit toilets are available; however, there is no water.

Ruins of the Cheney Estate

How to Get There: Access is by private boat only. The best access is on the western side of the island.

LITTLE CALF ISLAND

Lying 100 yards north of Calf Island is little Calf, a tiny outcrop of bedrock. Little Calf has never been inhabited by man, but is an active nesting area for cormorants. To preserve this nesting colony, public use of the island is not encouraged.

GREEN ISLAND

Lying just north of Little Calf, Green Island is a desolate two-acre rock outcropping covered with scrubby bushes and weeds. The island is named for Joseph Green, a well-known merchant who owned the island in colonial times. About the only human inhabitants of the island have been lobstermen and an occasional hermit. Since access is unsafe and the island is an active nesting area for gulls and cormorants, here too public use is discouraged. As you sail by the island, however, take a look at the erosion along its banks; this is in part due to the changes of ocean current patterns brought about by the dredging and filling of Boston Harbor.

SHAG ROCKS

Once known as Egg Rocks, Shag Rocks are a group of formidable bedrock ledges on which gulls and cormorants nest. Mariners are warned to take extra caution out here.

Shag Rocks with Boston Light in the Distance

THE GRAVES

The outermost light in Boston Harbor, Graves Light was built by the Federal Government in 1905 on a rocky outcrop known as Graves Ledge. The light marks the main entrance to Boston Harbor and the most northerly point of the Brewsters. The gray, 93-foot-high granite structure is manned by a keeper. Its beacon, flashing twice every six seconds, shines 16 miles out to sea.

The ledge was named for Thomas Graves, a vice-admiral in the fleet of seventeenth-century Massachusetts Governor John Winthrop. Over the years, the name has stuck, for it also evoked the shipwrecks that claimed so many lives off the ledges. It has even been said that the rocks look like headstones, marking the watery graves of the drowned.

While fancy may well have blurred into fiction, there is no doubt that there were countless wrecks off these treacherous shoals. Among a couple of latter-day disasters: in 1938, the *City of Salisbury*, carrying a cargo of wild animals, struck a submerged rock and sank with most of its cargo off the Graves. In 1941 during a winter gale, the fishing vessel *Mary E. O'Hara* hit a ledge west of the light. For hours the crewmen clung to masts swaying above the water until their hands froze and they succumbed to the icy seas.

Graves Light

Shipwrecks
of
Boston Harbor

45,000 SEAGULLS CAN'T BE WRONG

Boston Harbor offers a nearly ideal habitat for gulls. Many of the islands provide attractive sites for breeding colonies by virtue of their relative isolation, freedom from predators, and natural food sources. In addition, metropolitan Boston offers a nearby food subsidy—from wastes produced by human activity—that also lures these birds.

Gulls in the Greater Boston area are primarily herring gulls and black-backed gulls. There is evidence of nesting colonies on Green, Calf, Little Calf, Middle Brewster, Outer Brewster, Greater Brewster, Lovell's, Spectacle and Gallop's islands. Shallow nests loosely constructed of dried grasses and roughly a foot in diameter are tucked in among low-growing brush and debris on most of the islands. From May to July, mottled gray-green eggs are laid, followed by the appearance of downy chicks. The chicks rapidly grow to adult size, but are distinguished from adult gulls by their brown plumage.

The islands serve as gull graveyards as well as nurseries. The Brewsters, particularly Middle Brewster, which is primarily rocky terrain, are littered with dead gulls and bones. Getting onto Middle Brewster means climbing rocks covered with moss and slippery with viscous white gull droppings. Many grassy areas suitable for picnicking must be shared with old bones and birds in various stages of decomposition. These conditions are generally found on the sections of all islands where there are gull colonies.

Throughout the Eastern seaboard, major gull concentrations are found in metropolitan areas. In a winter census of gulls conducted from 1962 through 1964 (as reported in *Studies of Herring Gulls in New England*, prepared by the Massachusetts Audubon Society), 45,000 gulls were concentrated in Greater Boston alone. Of the 650,000 gulls censused (from Mexico to New Brunswick and Nova Scotia) in the winters of 1965 and 1967, over half—330,000—were observed in Greater Boston; Greater New York; Baltimore, Maryland; and Norfolk, Virginia. The Audubon Society study and the Metropolitan Area Planning Council's *Boston Harbor Islands Comprehensive Plan* provide much information on gulls and the problems they create, which we shall summarize here.

The average life expectancy of adult gulls is twelve years, and the population has been observed to increase at the rate of 5 percent per year over the last seventy years. The net result is that the herring gull population in New England has been doubling every twelve to fifteen years since 1900. At present, gulls are producing two to three times as many young as are balanced by mortality rates.

Studies have indicated that gulls at their breeding colonies eat a diet that is composed of half to three-quarters natural food such as mussels, crabs, clams, and small fish. The remainder of their food is essentially a subsidy composed of refuse from human activities:

garbage, fish wastes and sewage. Gulls congregate at food sources such as dumps, pig farms, sewage outfalls and fish piers, all of which are found in and around Boston Harbor. Studies of gull movement, and bird banding to trace migration patterns in relation to breeding colonies, show that gulls quickly abandon an area where food is no longer available and aggregate just as rapidly near a new food source. This movement is associated with natural food as well as food from refuse.

In recent years we have seen how human activity threatens many species of wildlife with extinction. But by subsidizing the gull we are tipping the natural balance in the opposite direction and creating potential hazards to our own population in the process.

Aside from the mere nuisance of increasing gull droppings on roofs, boats and piers, large gull populations seeking new breeding areas may force other bird colonies such as terns off their nesting grounds. In extreme cases, the gull population may eliminate nesting colonies of other birds in the Boston area by their aggressive behavior in establishing breeding colonies.

A far more serious hazard associated with our large gull population is the potential danger of an aircraft strike. In a study prepared by the Massachusetts Audubon Society for the Bureau of Sport Fisheries and Wildlife, and funded by the Federal Aviation Agency, it was concluded that gulls present the most serious hazard to aircraft at Logan International Airport.

The situation of Logan Airport in the Harbor, surrounded by mudflats, marshes and ponds, is itself an attraction to feeding and loafing birds. The proximity of other food sources such as fish piers, dumps and sewage outfalls makes bird trips across flight paths inevitable.

As the gull population increases, the potential for an aircraft strike rises. In its report, the Audubon Society records experiments with many methods of gull control including spraying eggs with formalin and oil mixtures, breaking eggs, killing gulls, inhibiting reproduction, introducing predators onto breeding colonies, and removing food subsidies. While a measure of success is possible using each method, or a combination of methods, only the removal of food subsidies will substantially reduce the gull population in a particular area and reduce the probability of gulls migrating in from other colonies. All other methods require a massive, well-run program, and they will need to be repeated at intervals to be effective and may threaten other wildlife if improperly administered.

The second major hazard posed by a large gull population is the potential for contamination of drinking water supplies. The water supply in the city of Gloucester was contaminated with salmonella and *Escherichia coli* bacteria in 1963, and fish have become contaminated by gulls carrying the bacteria and introducing them through their droppings. The presence of bacteria in gull droppings is a

potential health hazard to individuals using the islands for recreational purposes. It has been recommended that islands such as the Brewsters, whose sharp rocks are liberally covered with fresh gull droppings, be equipped with first-aid materials for prompt treatment of cuts and abrasions which may become infected from contact with gull droppings. Users of more remote islands, particularly campers, should treat skin injuries promptly to avoid infection.

Regular human use of the islands during the nesting season may have a discouraging effect on some breeding colonies. However, since the birds establish colonies in April and heavy use of the islands will probably not begin until June, a whole generation of new gulls may hatch before this control mechanism could have any effect.

All governmental agencies having regulatory powers over the disposal of edible wastes should be urged to demand compliance with the law. And more modern methods of handling fish and other wastes could eventually make refuse inaccessible to gulls.

Despite all these problems, however, the gulls—wheeling in arcs with their mournful cry—are an integral part of any seascape. They have colonized the islands naturally, and if their numbers can be controlled, it seems only fitting that the gulls remain part of the environment of the Harbor Islands.

HOMARUS AMERICANUS

Homarus americanus—the American lobster—is known as the King of Seafood. Fortunately for those with an insatiable appetite for the crustacean, the price of lobster sold in the summer has become more affordable in "real" dollars.

While most people associate lobsters with the rocky coast of Maine and Canada, they might be surprised to learn that the species is found in large numbers in Boston Harbor, especially off the Brewsters. In a recent study of the fishery in the Commonwealth, Gloucester ranked first, followed by Boston, Plymouth, and Fairhaven according to the number of total pounds caught. In 1991, 15,986,991 pounds of lobster were landed commercially in Massachusetts. The total value of the fishery, including boats, gear, and lobster, was $121,189,269. This figure places lobstering in first place in a ranking of economic values of fisheries in the Commonwealth.

Ever since man began fishing for lobster, he has gone about the job by piloting his rugged little boat along the coastline, dropping a few pots or traps into the water, and hauling in a modest catch the following day. Lobstering traditionally was a small-scale business—for the most part, a collection of one-man operations.

In recent years as the taste for lobster has grown, commercial lobstering has become a more elaborate affair. In order to meet the soaring demand, trawlers equipped with sophisticated gear and manned by several crewmen, were going far offshore for days to lay down long lines of pots. By 1991, nearly five million pounds of lobster, one-third of the annual Massachusetts catch, came from offshore waters.

The lobster stocks are healthy and are protected by several important conservation measures. The minimum allowable length of a lobster caught and held has actually increased through the years. The carapace length (distance from the back of the eye socket to back of the body shell) must be at least $3\frac{1}{4}$". Egg-bearing females are protected. Federal Management officials are now considering limited entry into the fishery.

The Fisheries Management Conservation Act passed in 1976 giving states jurisdiction over coastal waters to three miles and the federal government jurisdiction to 200 miles has also served to protect the lobster from exploitation by foreign vessels.

SOURCE: *1991 Massachusetts Lobster Fishery Statistics,* David McCarron and Thomas Hoopes, Massachusetts Division of Marine Fisheries

Gulls on the Tidal Flats

The Horseshoe Crab: An Inhabitant of the Intertidal Zone

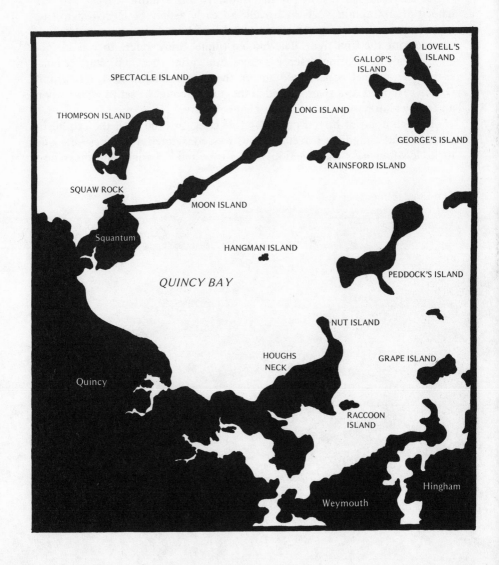

LOVELL'S
ISLAND

GALLOP'S
ISLAND

SPECTACLE ISLAND

LONG ISLAND

THOMPSON ISLAND

GEORGE'S ISLAND

RAINSFORD ISLAND

SQUAW ROCK

MOON ISLAND

Squantum

HANGMAN ISLAND

PEDDOCK'S ISLAND

QUINCY BAY

NUT ISLAND

HOUGHS
NECK

GRAPE ISLAND

Quincy

RACCOON
ISLAND

Hingham

Weymouth

LOVELL'S ISLAND

The Lovell's Island one encounters in the pages of Edward Rowe Snow is a romantic place indeed, complete with tales of buried pirate treasure, ill-fated lovers who froze to death locked in each other's arms on the island, and a secret tunnel leading to a mysterious fort. Then there is the wreck of the *Magnifique*, a French man-of-war that sunk off Lovell's in 1782. Snow claims that in this century gold and silver coin—perhaps that reputed to have gone down with the *Magnifique*—was found on Lovell's; and the Yankee yarn-spinner tantalizes us with the hint that maybe some of that treasure is still on the island.

But the recorded history of the island is much more prosaic. It was named after Captain William Lovell, an early settler of Dorchester. For most of its early history the island was farmed until it became a training camp during the Civil War. The hidden tunnel Snow refers to was in fact an elaborate submarine defense system built after the Civil War. It consisted of a tunnel constructed under the channel between Lovell's and Gallop's Island. Explosives, placed in the tunnel, could be set to go off when an enemy ship passed through the channel above.

The high point of Lovell's military role came in 1900 with the establishment of Fort Standish. Lovell's Island was considered a strategic site due to its location near the junction of the two main channel entrances into

Gun Emplacements on Lovell's

the Harbor—one leading into Dorchester Bay; the other, into Quincy Bay. The fort was named for Myles Standish, the early *Mayflower* arrival who was military leader of Plymouth Colony from 1620 to 1656. The remains of Fort Standish's gun batteries, bunkers and guardhouse still standing today offer a unique example of early twentieth-century military architecture; and they provide an interesting contrast with the earlier nineteenth-century architecture of Fort Warren on nearby George's Island.

Today the island, which is about three-quarters of a mile long and only one-quarter of a mile wide, offers several recreational possibilities, most notably stone and sand beaches which border some of the coldest—but cleanest—water in the Harbor. A word of caution to swimmers: currents on the westerly side of the island are strong, and it is considerably safer on the southerly side.

Facilities: Lovell's Island offers a boat and fishing pier, a swimming area, picnic tables and grills (no open fires), walking trails, individual and group campsites and portable toilets. Island managers are in residence from June to September. No water is available, and all trash must be carried off the island.

How to Get There: Access is by public water taxi from George's Island and by private boat. A pier is available for loading and unloading only. Permits are required for camping (for a nominal fee) and for day use by groups of 25 or more people. (See additional Park information, page 105.)

Docking Facility at Lovell's

Remains of Fortifications on Lovell's

Fort Warren, Visitor Center and Piers on George's Island

GEORGE'S ISLAND

The fateful shots fired at Fort Sumter in Charleston Harbor on April 12, 1861, reverberated in another harbor hundreds of miles to the north. Just two weeks after the Confederate attack, four companies of Massachusetts 2nd Infantry—the "Tiger Battalion"—landed at Fort Warren on George's Island to guard against a possible sea attack on Boston by the Southern rebels or their European allies.

True, the fort was hardly prepared for a major bombardment: there were practically no guns in readiness, and when Massachusetts Governor Andrew arrived at the island to wish the soldiers well, he had to wait until they could scrounge up enough ammunition to fire off the requisite salute.

The position of George's Island, right at the "throat" of Boston Harbor and facing the main ship channel, made it clearly the most important strategic point in the Harbor. However, it was our French allies in the Revolutionary War who first built earthwork fortifications on George's Island in 1778 to protect their fleet and the American colonists from the British.

Later, this strategic potential of George's Island (which had remained principally farmland since its original owner, James Pemberton, settled there back in 1628) was recognized by the U.S. Government, who sent Sylvanus Thayer—the "Father of West Point"—to oversee the construction of Fort Warren. The project, which began in 1833, took almost two decades to complete; each block of Quincy granite used to build the fort was cut and faced by hand, a process taking a single laborer two days to perform. (His munificent wage for this painstaking labor, by the way, was about forty-eight dollars per month!) But when it was finally finished, with ten-foot-thick walls, endless labyrinths of dungeon prisons and officers' quarters, a sweeping interior parade ground and massive parapets overlooking the sea, Fort Warren was indeed a formidable defense. One awestruck visitor, in fact, wrote that as a fortress, it surpassed even the Rock of Gibraltar.

The fort's real history, however, begins with those Massachusetts men of the Tiger Battalion. Their first task in that tense spring of 1861 was to clean out the rubble that had collected on the parade ground over the years. To help them pass the time during what was hardly an exciting military duty, the soldiers sang songs, among them a popular hymn, "Say, Brothers, Will You Meet Us?"

John Brown, a battalion member with the same name as the abolitionist who was hanged after the famous raid on Harper's Ferry two years earlier, joined in the fun and helped set lyrics about his namesake to the tune of this hymn. The song quickly spread through the ranks and caught on as the most stirring of Union marching songs; so much so that, according to several accounts, when President Lincoln heard it while visiting a Massachusetts regiment camped in Washington, he asked Julia Ward Howe to write a patriotic poem to the same melody. Thus "The Battle Hymn of the Republic," the most famous Civil War song outside of "Dixie," was born.

As the war effort grew, more and more boys from Massachusetts towns and farms arrived at George's Island to be trained for a few weeks or months before being sent South to their fates at the front lines. They drilled on Fort Warren's parade ground, in summer cooling off with a swim in the Harbor, or freezing in winter during snow patrols when icy winds lashed the island. There were complaints about the inevitable Army bean soup, but the soldiers were able to dig clams for chowder along the shore.

By the fall of 1861, however, the Federal Government decided to use Fort Warren for war captives. Overnight six hundred prisoners were landed on the island, many of them suspected Confederate sympathizers from the border state of Maryland as well as from places closer to home. The people of Boston rose to the occasion and helped meet the needs of the new arrivals with gifts of food, beds and other supplies. Humane treatment of the prisoners was the policy of the fort commander, Justin E. Dimmick, a deeply religious old soldier admired by Northerners and Southerners alike.

Life for the prisoners varied, depending on status, rank, and of course, financial resources. While enlisted men from North Carolina had to cook their own rations in improvised pots, members of the Maryland legislature

Aerial View of George's Island

lived in high style. One of them, Lawrence Sangston, recorded in his diary:

> At half-past four, when we leave the parade ground and retire to our rooms, . . . I trim and light my lamp, and prepare my writing table for those who wish to write, or read in quiet, leaving the front room for conversation, and the backgammon players. . . . At ten o'clock, I brew a pitcher of hot whiskey punch, which we sip until eleven; Colonel Pegram . . . gives us some very fine music from his guitar, and we put out the light and go to bed.

Hardly a life of deprivation and suffering. In fact, many Confederate officers and political prisoners were allowed to roam freely over George's Island, and to play football on the fort's parade grounds. Gifts and liquor from family and friends were also permitted, and there was even entertainment provided: fireworks displays on the Fourth of July, and the Cadet Ball, where several young soldiers—dressed in borrowed finery—took the place of the absent ladies.

Yet, even the most comfortable of prisons is still a prison, and there were several escape attempts—all of them abortive—during this period of Fort Warren's history. Perhaps the most elaborate was the scheme devised by four Confederate officers who squeezed through a narrow musketry loop-

Troops Garrisoned at Fort Warren during Civil War

hole in the fort. Two of them managed to swim across rough seas to Lovell's Island, where they picked up a boat and sailed north, only to be captured by a U.S. revenue cutter off the coast of Maine.

Among the prisoners interned at Fort Warren during the Civil War years were such contemporary luminaries as the police chief and future mayor of Baltimore; a major general and future governor of Missouri; and Confederate General Simon Bolivar Buckner. When Buckner, who had surrendered Fort Donelson to Ulysses S. Grant, was ordered into solitary confinement at George's Island, softhearted Commander Dimmick broke down and cried in sympathy. The result was that Buckner ended up consoling his jailer!

Perhaps the greatest stir was caused by the arrival at Fort Warren of two Confederate commissioners—James Murray Mason, a former U.S. senator, and his colleague, John Slidell. The two men were sailing on the British mail steamer *Trent* to Europe, seeking aid for the Southern cause, when a Union warship, the *San Jacinto*, intercepted the emissaries and brought them to George's Island. The event quickly boiled over into a *cause celebre*, and President Lincoln, fearful of an international incident which would push England into the war, arranged for Mason and Slidell's release. And so after little more than a month's detention in quarters so luxurious that Union guards were grumbling and jealous, the illustrious commissioners sailed off from George's Island.

Squad Room circa 1880, Formerly Used to House Prisoners of War

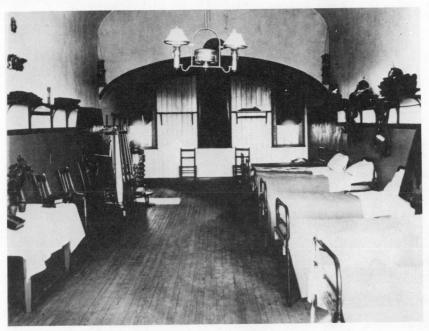

Not only international, but national politics affected events at Fort Warren throughout the Civil War. For one thing, since Lincoln had suspended certain constitutional rights during the national crisis, including habeas corpus, alleged conspirators and Confederate sympathizers were arrested and imprisoned without benefit of a trial. Thus many of the political prisoners at Fort Warren were the object of fierce moral and legal debates that raged throughout the country. Then too, as Lincoln worked out complicated prisoner-of-war exchanges with the South, those who had been interned at Fort Warren would depart, sometimes as suddenly as they had arrived. One group of prisoners released in the spring of 1862 celebrated their last night on George's Island with a farewell party that lasted through the night, dancing with the fort's laundry girls and drinking whiskey which "flowed like water."

Not surprisingly, Boston politics played a role in the fort's administration. Conscious of the inhumane treatment of prisoners of war at such notorious places as Andersonville, Bostonians had tried hard to maintain Fort Warren's reputation for human decency. But during Boston Mayor Wightman's reelection campaign, the voices criticizing his leniency toward the Southern prisoners grew louder. Instead of sending homemade jellies to the prisoners, fumed the mayor's opponents, such officials "ought themselves be pounded to a jelly in the municipal election."

Partly in response to this kind of feeling, the policy at Fort Warren tightened somewhat during the later war years; no gifts were allowed for a period, and troublemakers were summarily put in chains. When the vice president of the Confederacy, Alexander Stephens—arrested at his Georgia home soon after the fall of Richmond—arrived at George's Island one night in May 1865, he was first shorn of his money and papers, then confined alone in damp quarters in the cellar of the fort. Complaining of the damp and the poor rations he received, Stephens wrote in his journal of "the horrors of imprisonment, close confinement, no one to see or talk to . . . Words utterly fail to express the soul's anguish. This day I wept bitterly."

But a few months later Stephens was released from solitary confinement and was allowed to wander about the fort as he pleased. For other prisoners, with Lee's surrender at Appomattox and the general relaxation of tension that followed, life at Fort Warren had already begun to resume a more pleasant pace. Inmates were permitted to receive gifts once again, and there were also visits from Mary Salter, a young Boston belle who would sail by George's Island waving her handkerchief at the prisoners, to which the Confederate inmates would enthusiastically respond with a Rebel yell. (Miss Salter, by the way, married Alexander Stephens's half-brother, Linton Stephens.)

With the end of the Civil War, quiet returned to George's Island, broken only briefly by the Spanish-American War in 1898. Although the enemy never made an appearance in Boston Harbor, they were expected daily. Rumors were so prevalent, in fact, that one night there was a public banquet in Havana to celebrate the alleged "bombardment of Boston." One lookout stationed at Fort Warren, seeing four ships traveling single file, was sure it was the Spanish fleet at last. The "fleet" proved to be an ordinary tugboat towing three barges. The war did, however, serve to renew interest in Fort Warren as Boston's most important defense post, and efforts were made to strengthen fortifications with breech-loading rifles and mortars; soon after the war 3- and 4-inch guns were also mounted at the fort to protect against possible torpedo boats in Boston Harbor.

World War I saw yet another influx of soldiers; this time over sixteen hundred strong, arriving at George's Island for training before being sent over to France. At this time, also, the Harbor was mined against possible invading ships, and a mine control station was built at Fort Warren. As World War II approached, further gun emplacements were added. But except for one close call when a German U-boat neared the Harbor in World War II, the fort saw no real action during either global conflict.

The postwar history of George's Island is hauntingly familiar: as in the case of many of the forts in Boston Harbor which outlived their useful-ness, Fort Warren's guns were carted off to salvage yards, and the island was abandoned. Even though the fort has been designated a National Historic Site by the U.S. Department of the Interior, it has been the victim of both neglect and vandalism in recent years. No one knows quite how, but over three hundred chandeliers and hundreds of marble mantelpieces have been ripped down and spirited off George's Island; the elegant sconces and woodwork in the fort's once-luxurious apartments have also been stolen or destroyed.

Some restoration, however, is now in progress under the auspices of the MDC, which acquired George's Island in 1951. The crumbling murals of Civil War scenes on the walls of the John Brown Chapel have been restored. The famous apartments of Mason and Slidell and Alexander Stephens have been weatherproofed, and a crumbling seawall has just been replaced at a cost of almost $600,000. Other attractions planned by the MDC are

Cannons and Interior Grounds of Fort Warren after the Civil War

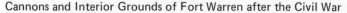

the restoration of the fort's bakery, of the Powder Magazine, and of the Administration Building. Living History exhibits and demonstrations are conducted on the island. Several highlights are the annual Civil War Encampment, featuring the reenactment of camp life, complete with military drills and authentic dress and the French Encampment, featuring regimental marching and 18th century clothing.

A Tale of George's Island

During past summers the late Harbor historian Edward Rowe Snow was often seen with a large group of tourists in tow. As he led them through the winding passages and dark tunnels of Fort Warren, Snow may well have related what has become the most popular "ghost story" of all the islands — "The Lady in Black."

According to one version of this legend, a young Confederate naval officer named Samuel Lanier was captured and imprisoned in Fort Warren's "corridor of dungeons." In a daring rescue attempt, his bride of a few weeks disguised herself as a man and, packing a pistol, rowed across to George's Island one stormy night. Although she managed to rendezvous with her husband at the prison, the two were discovered trying to dig an escape tunnel. Desperate, the wife aimed her pistol at Commander Dimmick, but it exploded, killing her husband instead. Our would-be heroine was sentenced to death as a spy, and chose for her hanging dress a robe made from the fort's black mess hall drapes. Ever since, so the story goes, the ghost of the Lady in Black has haunted Fort Warren, frightening away soldiers from their sentry duty during the long, lonely night. And apocryphal though the tale may be, as the wind howls through Fort Warren's mysterious corridors and turrent staircases, echoing in its vaulted chambers and dungeon cells, all the ghosts of the Civil War still seem very much alive.

Fort Warren.

Servicemen in the Fort's Bakery, 1944

The Bakery in the 1970's, before Restoration

Facilities: Only day use is permitted. Facilities include picnic tables, grills (no open fires), litter barrels, a first aid station, and portable toilets (located outside the fort). Swimming is discouraged. A concession sells food, drinks and souvenirs. Seasonal program staff offer visitor information, educational displays and tours of Fort Warren. Groups of 25 or more must apply for a permit from the M.D.C. Water is available. No alcohol is permitted on the Harbor Islands.

How to Get There: From April through October, several commercial boat lines make daily trips between downtown Boston and George's Island. Boat lines can be reached by the M.B.T.A.—Aquarium or South Station stops. There is also seasonal boat service to George's Island from the Lynn Heritage State Park (598-1974) and the Hingham Shipyard.

George's Island is the departure point for public water taxi service to Gallop's, Lovell's, Grape, Bumpkin, and Peddock's Islands in the Boston Harbor Islands State Park. There are occasional day trips to Calf and Great Brewster Islands. Visitor information and boat schedules are provided at the Park information booth. The MDC offers limited dockage space for private boats at no charge. (See Park Information page 105).

GALLOP'S ISLAND

Like so many of the Boston Harbor Islands, Gallop's Island was abandoned after World War II and entered into a period of decay, only used occasionally as a dump. Today, the decay has been arrested and restoration has begun. Debris has been removed, old buildings demolished, and the island's general appearance improved.

The 16-acre Gallop's—which lies just west of Lovell's and George's islands at the entrance to Quincy Bay—offers a pleasant outdoor experience with a sandy beach, a profusion of wild roses in summertime and a grassy knoll that commands fine views of the entire Harbor, especially Boston Light and the Boston skyline. From this knoll the visitor can observe the gulls nesting on the seawalls or muse over Edward Rowe Snow's claim that somewhere on Gallop's the diamond treasure of the notorious pirate "Long Ben" Avery still lies buried, waiting to be discovered—maybe by you.

Pier on Gallop's Island

The island was named after its first owner, Captain John Gallop, a Harbor pilot. It was farmed extensively in the eighteenth and early nineteenth centuries. From the 1830's until the Civil War, the island was a popular resort featuring an inn and restaurant famous for its good chowder.

During the Civil War, three thousand soldiers were encamped on the island. After the war, the island was the site of a quarantine hospital; then an immigration station was added in 1916. Right before World War II, the U.S. Maritime Service established a radio school on the island. After that war, the buildings were dismantled.

From his perch atop Gallop's knoll these days, the visitor will also have a good view of Nix's Mate, lying just north of the island. At one time a fairly sizable island, Nix's Mate is today little more than a channel marker, dominated by a black-and-white-striped cement pyramid, as its shifting sands have washed away over the years. No one really knows how Nix's Mate got its name. But the best theory advanced is that Gallop's Island was once owned by a man named Nix and the smaller island, also owned by Nix, came to be know as Nix's Mate. In any event, the island has the dubious distinction of once being the burial site of pirates, whose corpses were often first hung in chains to be, in the words of an eighteenth-century chronicler, "a spectacle for the Warning of Others."

Facilities: Gallop's Island offers trails, picnic areas, a sandy shoreline, pit toilets, and spectacular views. Island managers are in residence from June to September. Day-use permits are required for groups of 25 or more people. (See additional Park information, page 105.) No water is available, and all trash must be carried off the island.

How to Get There: Access is by public water taxi from George's Island and by private boat. There are no docking facilities; a pier is available for loading and unloading only.

Lovell's Island and the Brewsters, from Gallop's Island.

MOON ISLAND

The unsuspecting visitor to Moon Island—the connecting link between Long Island and the mainland—may be startled by the sudden appearance of firefighters scaling a wall, or the crack of pistol fire. He will be relieved to learn that the island has been used in recent years by the Boston Fire Department and the Boston and Quincy police departments. The fire department conducts firefighting classes at the northern end of the island, practicing on a concrete building that is designed to simulate the various roof shapes and window types found in Boston. And down on the southern end of Moon Island, the police department operates a pistol training and practice range.

A visitor can watch these practice and training activities if they happen to be in session. Or he can hike to the top of the hill, 100 feet above sea level, where a commanding view can be had of Quincy and Dorchester Bay, Squantum, the Harbor Islands, the Blue Hills and the city skyline. But the best attraction of Moon is fishing. There is good fishing for flounder, mackerel and striped bass along the western shoreline and particularly from the granite seawall on the northern end.

A little-known footnote to Moon Island's history is that it was hailed by experts of the day as having the best sewage disposal system in the world. That was back in 1878, when the City of Boston began construction of a brick sewer system running from Boston to Squantum, under Dorchester Bay and out to Moon Island under the causeway. Four huge granite storage tanks, with a capacity of 50 million gallons, were constructed on Moon as a reservoir to hold raw sewage. The gates to the reservoir were opened twice daily on the outgoing tide and the sewage flowed into the Harbor. This gigantic project, which was completed in 1884, cost the City of Boston $6 million. In recent years, the Deer Island and Nut Island sewage treatment facilities have taken over the job of sewage disposal. But the storage tanks, now empty, still remain.

Facilities: Asphalt-paved parking area.

How to Get There: By auto from Squantum, Quincy, over two-lane causeway.

A FISH STORY

Although it is underutilized, Boston Harbor has good fishing. Fishermen say their luck is always pretty good off any wharf, pier or jetty, except in the Inner Harbor where pollution makes it undesirable.

The best fishing is generally where the deep water comes near shore. Among a few top spots: the pier at Castle Island and along the shore, Commercial Point near the Boston Gas tanks in Dorchester, off the Columbia Point campus of the University of Massachusetts, and Moon Island.

The best fish to catch—and to eat—are flounder, striped bass, mackerel (best fishing from May to October) and cod (best fishing in fall, spring and winter).

No license is required for saltwater fishing in Massachusetts. (See Directory for where to go fishing, bait and tackle shops, boat rentals and charter boats.) Beginners can get advice on what type of fish to catch and equipment to use from bait and tackle shops and can pick up other pointers from fellow fishermen. Some of the most popular sport fish in Boston Harbor are:

Cod

Cod—The symbol of Massachusetts is the "sacred cod," and a gold codfish hangs in the Massachusetts State House testifying to its vital role in the development and trade of the Commonwealth. So important was the cod that it was one of the first natural resources in colonial America to be protected by a conservation law. In 1639 the Massachusetts Bay Colony ordered that no cod could be used as fertilizer for farm crops.

The cod is no less in demand today than it was in colonial times. In fact, because of its appealing taste and texture, it is overfished commercially, particularly by foreign fleets lying off the New England coast. As a result, cod stocks have been dangerously declining in the northwest Atlantic in recent years.

The codfish can be identified by its streamline shape, three dorsal fins, square tail and small chin whisker. Its color ranges from gray to gray-green, to brick-red to almost black. The upper part of the cod is marked with spots and a prominent light horizontal line. Cod caught in Boston Harbor average around three pounds and measure about twenty inches long.

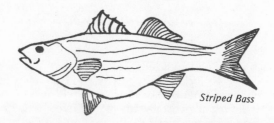

Striped Bass

Striped Bass—Ranks only second to the immortal cod as a vital marine resource in early American history. Like the cod, striped bass could not be ground up and used as fertilizer for farm crops in colonial times. Another historical note is that the first public (free) school in the New World was made possible through funds derived in part from the sale of striped bass. And a portion of the funds was also used to help widows and orphans of men formerly employed in service to the colony.

The striped bass has also been a favorite of sport fishermen since colonial times. One early historian called the fish "the boldest, bravest, strongest and most active fish that visited tidal waters and bays along the Atlantic Seaboard."

The striped bass is an anadromous fish, meaning it ascends rivers (from March to July) to spawn and then returns to the sea. It can be recognized by olive-green stripes that run lengthwise across its body. Striped bass found in the Harbor average from three to five pounds and twenty inches in length; but they can run up to ten or fifteen pounds and three feet long.

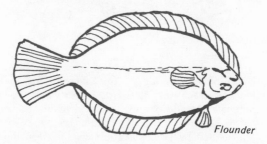

Flounder

Flounder—The yellowtail and winter flounder are the two principal flounder species found in Boston Harbor. As members of the flatfish family rather bizarre in appearance, flounders are sometimes called the "clowns of the sea."

A flounder is born upright with normally placed eyes. But then its skull begins to twist and one eye moves toward the other side. At the same time, the fish begins to tilt. Within a short time, both eyes peer from the same side and the fish swims with the eyeless side down.

As they ripple and glide through the water, flounders resemble flying saucers. Part of nature's camouflage is the way they glide to the bottom and then flip sand over their backs, becoming almost invisible except for their protruding eyes.

When a small fish or other prey is spotted, the flounder, with a squirt of water from the underside gill jet, propels itself off the bottom in hot pursuit. The white belly side blends with light filtering down through the water, protecting it from enemies below. The darker topside usually resembles the color of the bottom on which the flounder lives.

But unfortunately for the flounder, its protective coloration and other adaptive devices for survival are not always enough. For its firm, white delicate flesh makes it one of the finest of all food fish and one avidly sought after by both anglers and commercial fishermen. Flounders average between twelve ounces and one pound and measure ten to fourteen inches.

Mackerel

Mackerel—Known also as the Atlantic or Boston mackerel, this fish belongs to the same family as the tuna. With its jolting strikes, breakneck runs and stubborn struggling, it also offers anglers a battle similar to that put up by the tuna.

Mackerel are prolific, but many factors affect survival of the young. Eggs are released wherever the fish happen to be, and adverse winds may push eggs or small fry into areas where survival chances are slight. This, combined with numerous predators that feed on mackerel, accounts for a curious pattern of either scarcity or superabundance of the species.

Mackerel can be identified by their smooth, tapering heads, streamlined bodies and brilliant coloration in the water. (Their colors fade in the supermarket.) Iridescent greenish-blue covers most of the upper body, turning to blue-black on the head and silvery-white on the belly. Mackerel found in the Harbor weigh from one and a quarter to two and a half pounds and measure from fourteen to eighteen inches long.

LONG ISLAND

Long Island has been both greatly endowed by nature and considerably blighted by man. The largest island in the Harbor, its 213 acres are tantalizingly close to Boston—linked to Moon Island by a steel bridge, and via Moon to Squantum on the mainland. Marshes and thick pine woods, apple trees, sumac and sapling poplars harbor a flourishing wildlife population, most notably rabbits and birds. As an added attraction, several sand and gravel beaches offer good swimming possibilities.

Amidst all this natural beauty, however, stands the Long Island Chronic Disease Hospital, a grim complex of about twenty buildings sprawled over sixty acres of the island. Nearby is a cemetery with two thousand unmarked graves, formerly used as a potter's field by the hospital. The hospital was closed in May of 1991. The City of Boston operates a homeless shelter in one of the old buildings.

This history dates back to 1882, when the City of Boston first purchased a large hotel, built during the island's earlier heyday as a resort, and converted it into an almshouse for six hundred and fifty paupers. In 1921 it was turned into a home and hospital for unwed mothers. A dormitory for homeless men was built in 1928, and in 1941 a facility for three hundred alcoholics was added. Over the years, parts of the hospital failed to meet fire and safety codes, as well as public health licensing requirements.

But there is more to Long Island's history than this rather depressing saga. For one thing, there is Long Island Light, built in 1819 and still

Lighthouse and Bunker at Long Island Head

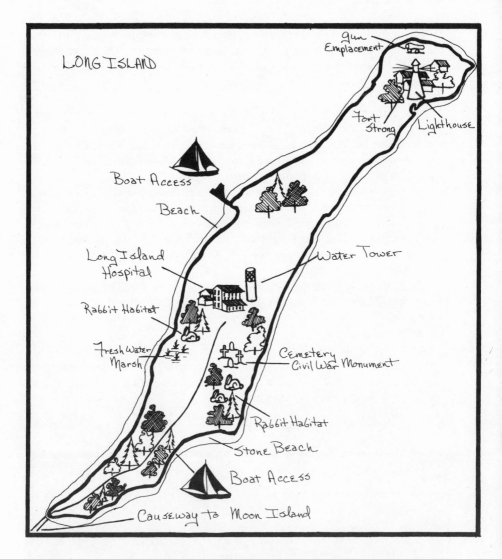

LONG ISLAND

gun Emplacement

Fort Strong

Lighthouse

Boat Access

Beach

Long Island Hospital

Water Tower

Rabbit Habitat

Fresh Water Marsh

Cemetery Civil War Monument

Rabbit Habitat

Stone Beach

Boat Access

Causeway to Moon Island

standing on the hill at the far end of the island. (Today this unmanned lighthouse is run by the Coast Guard.) Sharing Long Island Head with the lighthouse are the crumbling bunkers and batteries of Fort Strong. In addition, the remains of a gun battery, constructed just before the outbreak of the war, still can be seen, and there is a memorial to seventy nine Civil War dead in a cemetery located on the southern end of the island.

During the Civil War the island became an important conscript camp. By 1863, there were several companies of heavy artillery and about a thousand draftees. The camp was named Camp Wightman, after Boston's mayor, and after the war it was the scene of countless illicit prizefights.

In 1867, Fort Strong was moved here from another island. (The fort was named in honor of Major General George C. Strong, who was killed at Fort Wagner, South Carolina, in 1863.) During extensive renovation of Fort Strong in 1899, batteries of six- and 12-inch guns were emplaced. Later, in the First World War, fifteen hundred men were quartered at the fort. But by World War II the guns were obsolete, and although the fort was used as a mine operations center, it was closed down right after the war. And with that, the period of decay began.

The final postscript to the island's military history was a Nike missile base set up in the early 1950's during the cold war. The Russians never came, and the underground silos housing the missiles were abandoned a number of years ago. But since that time the silos have been used to provide temporary storage space for—of all things—700,000 volumes from the Boston Public Library.

Archeologists working on the island have discovered a 9,000-year-old spear-point, the oldest artifact found in the Boston area. Indians lived on Long Island for centuries until local farmers petitioned to have them removed at the start of the King Philip's War.

In spite of its natural beauty and historical significance, Long Island is not open to the public. Only those visitors conducting official business or bringing donations to the shelter are admitted. Any person trying to access the island from the beach is turned away by the guards.

The Long-Island House.

RAINSFORD ISLAND

Rainsford, lying just off Long Island, is a small island of 11 acres. Its dominant feature, a drumlin at one end, gives the island a gentle sloping profile. It was originally granted to Edward Rainsford about 1636 for use as a farm.

Rainsford's subsequent history is a macabre mixture running the gamut from merriment to death. In 1737 the quarantine hospital was moved from Spectacle Island to Rainsford. But the island had also become a popular summer resort; so an inn, which had been established there, was allowed to take in boarders whenever no communicable diseases were reported at the hospital. One can imagine the pall that descended on the island when an outbreak occurred, followed by a great carousing and the clinking of ale tankards when the all-clear signal was given.

One of the hospital buildings, ambitiously constructed in 1832 in the style of a Greek temple, was a smallpox facility. Hundreds of those who died from this and other diseases were buried on the island. Before the tombstones were removed to Long Island some years ago, Edward Rowe Snow noted a number of their epitaphs. Two of these grim reminders of man's mortality:

NEARBY THESE GRAY ROCKS
ENCLOSED IN A BOX
LIES HATTER COX
WHO DIED OF SMALLPOX

BEHOLD AND SEE AS YOU PASS BY
AS YOU ARE NOW, SO ONCE WAS I
AS I AM NOW, SO YOU MUST BE
PREPARE FOR DEATH AND FOLLOW ME

Checking for Smallpox

The Port Physician boarding an Inbound
Ship.

The later history of the quarantine hospital offers an insight into Victorian notions of social reform. When in 1852 the hospital closed down, it was converted first into a state almshouse and then, after the Civil War, into the city poorhouse. Several Civil War veterans lived on the island until 1882, when they were transferred to the Soldiers Home in Chelsea, and the next residents were "female paupers"—a nineteenth-century version of sexist discrimination, perhaps.

The institution was later reorganized as a reformatory and in 1895 became known as the Suffolk School for Boys. The boys were transferred to other detention centers in 1920 and the antiquated facilities were permanently shut down. Today all that remains of this sad succession of hospitals, poorhouses and detention buildings are a few foundation ruins.

Instead, Rainsford offers a quiet maritime experience. You can sit on a grassy knoll, gazing off toward the mainland and the Blue Hills in the far distance; toward Hull peninsula and other islands of Boston Harbor; or up toward the sky where a hawk might be circling the island in search of some unsuspecting prey below. During the spring and late summer you can see the sandpiper, in its inimitable comic manner, running before the waves and pecking in the sand for insects and crustaceans. There is good flounder fishing offshore.

Facilities: Only day use is permitted. There is no water available, and all trash must be carried off the island.

How to Get There: Access is by private boat only. There are plans to build a pier at Rainsford Island, but at present the best access is by either of two small natural coves on the south and southwest part of the island.

Rainsford Island.

View of Rainsford

ISLAND FLORA

The Harbor Islands as a whole contain a wide range of vegetation. In addition to Peddock's, other islands like Thompson and Long Island offer an especially great variety. Here is a brief description of the most common trees and shrubs found on the islands.

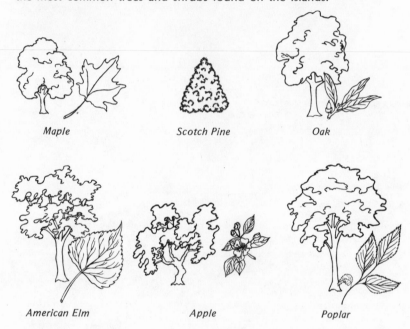

Maple   Scotch Pine   Oak

American Elm   Apple   Poplar

TREES

Maple—Widely native to eastern North America. Displays gorgeous autumn colors of yellow, orange and scarlet.

Scotch Pine—Found on several islands either as an isolated tree or in groups. Good tree for withstanding harsh seashore environment. During the Great Depression the Civilian Conservation Corps (CCC) planted 100,000 pine trees on the islands. But many of them were cut down in World War II to clear the way for fortifications.

Apple—Scattered over several of the islands. Colorful blossoms in the spring. Provides food for birds in the fall. Apples suitable for cooking.

Poplar—Found both scattered and in dense thickets throughout most of the islands.

Peach and Pear—Both varieties found on a few islands. Provide colorful autumn foliage and fruit for birds in the fall.

Chokeberry—Found everywhere in eastern North America as a weed tree. Fall fruits provide food for birds.

Oak—Large and long-lived. Excellent ornamental tree. Red autumn foliage. Acorns provide fall and winter food for small animals.

American Elm—Graceful, vase-like form, but susceptible to the Dutch elm disease.

Poison Ivy

Rugosa Rose

Beach Plum

SHRUBS

Bayberry—Found in clumps on several islands. Grows in poor sandy soils and withstands saltwater spray. Provides fall and winter food for birds. Settlers in colonial times used the wax from berries for candle-making.

Poison Ivy—This poisonous shrubby vine is found on most of the islands. Its only virtue is its white berries that provide food for birds. It may be identified by its clusters of three shiny leaves.

Staghorn Sumac—Dominant vegetation on all the Harbor Islands. The sumac grows rapidly and thrives in poor soils, often reaching the size of a small tree. The fruits, small, reddish and borne in tight clusters, provide food for birds.

Rugosa Rose—Commonly called salt spray rose, wild rose or rose hips. An import from Asia. Shrub of upright thick stems covered with hair-like spines. Leaves are coarse and shiny. Blossoms are purplish-red and white. Seems to thrive on salt spray and fog. An unconfirmed story has it that a cargo ship bound for Boston carrying seeds and rose plants ran aground on Cape Cod. The seeds and plants, packed in crates in the hold, washed ashore where they took root and spread up and down the coast to Boston Harbor and beyond.

Raspberry and Blackberry—These two shrubs produce dense, thorny thickets in many places on the islands, providing a haven for birds. Fruits are edible.

Beach Plum—Woody shrub that has twisted and gnarled trunks growing to heights of 18 to 30 inches. Its roots spread horizontally. Blossoms in May and June have purple-tinged center, turning purple throughout as the flowers die. By autumn the berries, about the size of a small cherry, turn purple when ripe. Beach plum jelly, a New England favorite, is made from the berries.

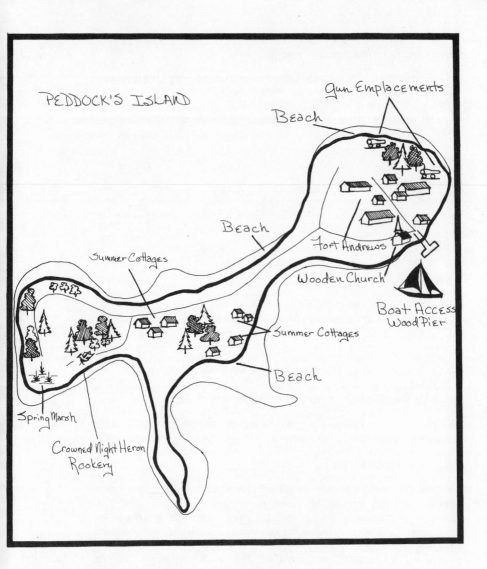

PEDDOCK'S ISLAND

Gun Emplacements

Beach

Beach

Summer Cottages

Fort Andrews

Wooden Church

Boat Access
Wood Pier

Summer Cottages

Beach

Spring Marsh

Crowned Night Heron
Rookery

PEDDOCKS ISLAND

The unique topography and natural beauty of Peddocks Island, combined with its rich social and military history, offer the visitor an unforgettable island experience. Wear your walking shoes and get ready to explore!

Peddocks has the longest shoreline of the harbor islands. Because of the formation of multiple drumlins (Heads) early in its history, Peddocks is often described as four islands in one.

The pier and the historic ruins of Fort Andrews are located on East Head. Grape and Bumpkin Islands combined are just equal to the size of East Head. There is a main trail across East Head to Middle, Prince, and West Heads. Visitors walk on sandy trails, through maple groves and grassy paths to Middle Head, nicknamed Middle Island. This part of the island has been inhabited since the late 1800's. Many Portuguese fishing families floated their homes across to Peddocks from Long Island, where they were displaced due to construction activity. All areas and trails on Middle Head are accessible to the public. There is a salt marsh which attracts a wide variety of bird life.

From Middle Head, continue your exploration around Prince Head and on to West Head. Today, Prince Head is an eroding bluff that extends into Hingham Bay. The visitor should note that it is covered with poison ivy. The West Head of Peddocks is a wildlife sanctuary and contains a brackish freshwater pond.

A small white church, its spare wooden lines reminiscent of early New England, stands near the dock, and has been used by a local Roman Catholic priest for services for the island's summer residents. In striking contrast to this modest building are the numerous elaborate, architecturally ornate structures that one discovers in various stages of decay on the eastern end of Peddock's Island. These are the remains of Fort Andrews, a sprawling complex built in 1900 by the U.S. Government in the wake of concern—stirred by the Spanish-American War—for Boston's harbor defense system.

During the First World War, the fort was garrisoned by coastal artillery; in World War II antiaircraft guns and observation stations were

The Appealing White Church on Peddocks Island

added. Fort Andrews was also used as a prison to hold over a thousand Italian prisoners of war during World War II. The observant visitor will discover memorabilia of this era in a mural of a prison scene, painted on a wall of a collapsing, POW barracks. Most of the fort's buildings—guardhouse, quartermaster storehouse, stable, gymnasium and firehouse—are still standing, although in many cases, just barely. Hurricanes which hit the Massachusetts coast in the mid-1950's furthered the destruction of many buildings.

The fort is surrounded by one of the most densely wooded areas of Boston Harbor. In striking contrast to the manicured sloping banks which first greet one on landing at Peddock's, here are cool, thick forests of mature and sapling maple, pine, apple, birch and cottonwood trees and beautiful viburnum shrubs. Fort Andrews is situated in a valley between two wooded hills (both drumlins) in the eastern part of the island. Along the old asphalt paths that wind through the fort area, maple, pine, apple and birch trees grow. The island's sandpits support beach plum and large clumps of wild roses.

On the undeveloped western section of Peddock's (also a drumlin) the range of vegetation is completed. Here grasses, milkweed and cattails in a small salt marsh contrast with the mature maples, poplars and pines found on the eastern end. Paths run through dense brush and trees. A black-crowned night heron rookery—reported by the Massachusetts Audubon Society to be one of the only two such rookeries in the entire state—is located right here amid a clump of apple trees.

A few years back, in 1971, a summer resident on Peddock's named Josephine Walsh made a startling discovery while digging in her backyard: the skeleton of an Indian man who lived, according to a carbon-dating study, 4100 years ago. The skeleton, the oldest ever found in New England, caused quite an archaeological sensation.

Facilities: Camping is permitted by permit only; there are formal camp sites. Bring your own drinking water, although there is water available on the island in the event of an emergency. There are toilet facilities. Dirt and asphalt paths extending throughout the island offer opportunities for hiking and nature study. The different kinds of structures on the island including the brick guardhouse, prisoner barracks and officers' quarters of Fort Andrews and the old wooden church, offer historic interest. Resident island staff provide tours of Fort Andrews, but visitors are cautioned to stay out of any buildings not on the tour, as many are on the verge of collapse.

Officers' Quarters, Fort Andrews

For group outings and camping permits, contact the M.D.C. Harbor Region at 727-5290. All trash must be carried off the island.

How to Get There: A public water taxi runs from Georges Island to Peddocks. There has also been seasonal boat service from the Hingham Shipyard directly to Peddocks Island. There are no docking facilities. A pier is available for loading and unloading only.

When you arrive at Peddocks, check in at the visitor center to receive a free trail map of the island.

HANGMAN ISLAND

Located far out in Quincy Bay west of Peddock's Island, Hangman Island is one of the smallest islands in Boston Harbor. In fact, this quarter-acre barren rock outcrop with a small pebble beach on the south side is little more than a sea-washed reef. The island serves as a loafing area for gulls, ducks, cormorants and other seabirds. It is speculated that the island's name is derived from pirate days when it was used for executions.

Camping Area, Peddock's Island

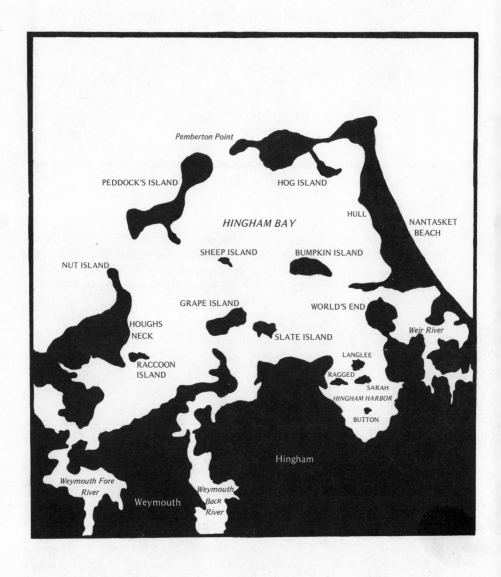

Pemberton Point

PEDDOCK'S ISLAND

HOG ISLAND

HULL

HINGHAM BAY

NANTASKET
BEACH

NUT ISLAND

SHEEP ISLAND

BUMPKIN ISLAND

GRAPE ISLAND

WORLD'S END

Weir River

HOUGHS
NECK

SLATE ISLAND

LANGLEE

RACCOON
ISLAND

RAGGED

SARAH

HINGHAM HARBOR

BUTTON

Hingham

Weymouth Fore
River

Weymouth
Back
River

Weymouth

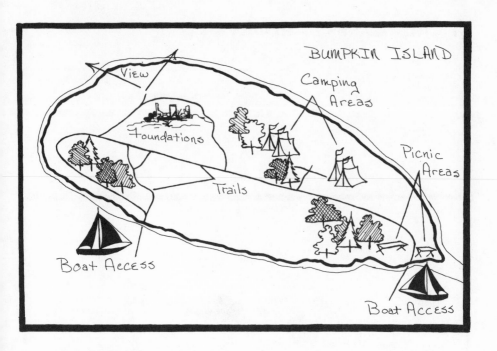

BUMPKIN ISLAND

To the boater landing at Bumpkin Island just about sunset, the sight of its picturesque stone ruins against the brilliant sky is sure to remind him of some romantic Greek isle. In actuality, however, the history of this island —located just a few hundred yards northwest of Sunset Point in Hull—

Ruins on Bumpkin

is quite unspectacular. Originally a farm, it was donated by owner Samuel Ward to Harvard College in 1682; Harvard, in turn, rented the island to tenant farmers until 1900. At that point, a local philanthropist bought the island and built a hospital for paraplegic children. To better accommodate its patients, who numbered as many as 145 children, the hospital was designed with ramps instead of stairs.

With the outbreak of World War I, however, the U.S. Navy took over Bumpkin, stationing thirteen hundred men there by 1918. After the war the Navy tore down its temporary structures, but the hospital remained. However, it was never reopened and was destroyed by fire in 1945. And it is these remaining foundations and walls of the hospital which are Bumpkin's romantic "crumbling ruins."

Facilities: Bumpkin Island offers informal picnic areas and walking trails with fine views of Hingham Bay and surrounding communities. Family campsites are available for a fee of $5.00 and group picnic sites for a fee of $16.00. To reserve a site, register two weeks in advance through Park Headquarters. (See Additional Park Information, page 105.) Island managers are in residence from June through September. No water is available, and all trash must be carried off the island.

How to Get There: Access is by public water taxi from Georges Island and the Hingham Shipyard and by private boat. There are no docking facilities. A pier is available for loading and unloading only.

Bumpkin Island

GRAPE ISLAND

Named for the abundance of grapes that flourished on the island in colonial times, the island is situated in Hingham Bay just five hundred yards from the mainland town of Weymouth.

The island consists of two large drumlins with a depression of land between them. The west drumlin—the larger of the two, rising more than 70 feet above sea level—offers a panorama of the coastline and the Harbor. And the irregular topography of this compact 50-acre island provides excellent walking or jogging trails.

Vegetation consists mainly of wild grasses, sumac shrubs and a few trees. Red raspberries, blackberries and wild roses heighten the foliage color in summer and provide food for birds and other fowl like quail and pheasant.

The northern shore is rocky, while the southern side facing the mainland has tidal salt marshes and several gravel swimming beaches.

During the Revolution the island was reputed to be the site of a skirmish known as the Battle of Grape Island, a somewhat grandiose name, since it isn't very likely that the incident significantly affected the outcome of the Revolution. According to Edward Rowe Snow, the eminent chronicler of Boston Bay, it all started when Elisha Levitt, a prominent Tory who owned the island, offered hay to the British army for their horses quartered in Boston. When the Redcoats went to gather the hay on May 21, 1775, South Shore Minutemen intercepted the foraging party—either on Grape Island itself or across on the mainland—and sent them packing.

Grape, like so many of the other islands, has attracted misfits, hermits and a fair share of fugitives from justice. One such personality was a notorious character named Captain Smith, whose real name was Amos Pendleton. Pendleton, we are told, was a slave-runner who became a smuggler after the Civil War. When things got too hot down in the Louisiana bayous, Pendleton fled to New England with the law on his heels and settled on Grape. There he set himself up like a little despot, shooting at anyone who trespassed on his island. Pendleton eventually died in 1897 at the age of ninety-two in a Hingham poorhouse.

Ever since colonial times the island has been farmed. In fact, it probably was plowed with oxen that were walked out over land that once connected the island with the mainland. A sandspit off the island is still discernible.

Before the white man arrived, the Indians farmed the island and dug clams from its tidal flats. These days, you may come upon another kind of "dig," because archaeologists have recently combed Grape for clues to how the Indians utilized the Harbor Island resources. They have already uncovered a number of middens—piles of clamshells which are the Indians' version of a garbage dump.

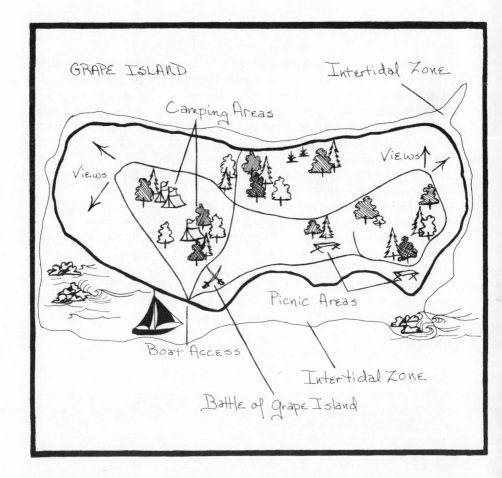

GRAPE ISLAND

Intertidal Zone

Camping Areas

Views

Views

Picnic Areas

Boat Access

Intertidal Zone

Battle of Grape Island

The fact that Grape, unlike many of the other Harbor Islands, was not disturbed by construction of military installations makes significant archaeological discoveries quite possible. In addition, the salt marshes surrounding the island act as a sort of preservative for artifacts from some earlier time buried under the muck and water.

Facilities: Grape Island offers walking trails and picnic areas. Family campsites and group picnic sites are available. To reserve a site, register two weeks in advance through Park Headquarters. (See Additional Park Information, page 105.) Island managers are in residence from June through September. No water is available; however, there are pit toilets. All trash must be carried off the island.

How to Get There: Access is by public water taxi from George's Island and the Hingham Shipyard, and by private boat. There are no docking facilities; a pier is available for loading and unloading only.

SLATE ISLAND

Located just east of Grape Island, 12-acre Slate is certainly aptly named. The island is essentially a series of slate ledges; some jutting out into the water, others forming steep cliffs along the shore. And tiny particles and flakes of slate form a small beach on the southwest corner of the island.

As early as 1650, the island was quarried for slate. Although the island's fine, soft rock was not suited for roofing material, it was used for cellar walls and underpinnings. Quarries (which you still can see today) were located along the northwest side of the island, where ships would anchor offshore, waiting to load the slate.

But for one hermit, who was said to have lived on the island in the nineteenth century, Slate was largely uninhabited over the years. A summer camp for boys was set up from 1937 to 1939, but closed because of a lack of sanitary facilities.

Dense brush covering most of the island provides a habitat for birds. Thorny thickets of raspberry and barberry shrubs also provide food for the birds. The explorer should be cautioned, however, that there is an abundance of poison ivy. Other vegetation consists of wild roses, a few trees and sumac.

Facilities: Some poison ivy has been cleared and walking trails have been laid out so that slate quarries can be observed.

How to Get There: Access by boat only. Best approach is the beach on the southwest corner of the island. Like Grape, Slate Island is readily accessible by rowboat.

SHEEP ISLAND

Here before your eyes is a dramatic example of the forces of erosion. Once covering an area of more than 25 acres, Sheep Island has been whittled down over the centuries to a long, narrow two-acre sliver of land only a few feet above sea level. It lies between Peddock's Island on the north and Grape Island on the south.

In colonial times the island was used as a sheep pasture. During the nineteenth century, it was visited by camping parties and duck hunters. Covered with grass and a variety of brush, Sheep is constantly being eroded by winds and sea. Because of its size and limited use, visiting the island is discouraged.

RACCOON ISLAND

Three-acre Raccoon Island, a tiny bedrock outcropping, lies just off Manet Beach on Hough's Neck in Quincy. Outcroppings on the north side of the island rise to an elevation of 30 feet above the surrounding bay. Mudflats, gravel beaches and rocky slopes create a wide variety of marine habitats, such as the small patches of eelgrass that provides protection and nourishment for ducks, geese and a variety of small sea animals.

Eelgrass is the only plant that has roots, stems, leaves and grows under salt water. Snails and plankton feed on its decaying parts, while crabs hunt for food among its roots. Examining a piece of washed-up eelgrass when it is dark green and wet you may find clinging to it other plant-like animals, tube worms in white coils, or even other seaweed—all of which indicate a flourishing plant and animal community just offshore.

There is little recorded history of activity on Raccoon Island. However, in the 1930's, the Stigmatine Order is known to have conducted summer school on the island. Nowadays, summer months find adventurous kids swimming over from the Quincy shore to explore the island. There is conclusive evidence that native Americans used the island as a summer campsite.

Facilities: None contemplated. The island will remain in its natural state.

How to Get There: By private boat only.

NUT ISLAND

Once a four-acre island, Nut Island is now a man-made peninsula, about 17 acres in size and attached to Quincy on the mainland. The peninsula, along with Hull, form the pincers that separate Quincy Bay from Hingham Bay. In colonial times cattle grazed on the island and were driven back to the mainland over a sandbar at low tide.

In 1876, a foundry company established a testing site on the island for heavy ordnance. Huge 15-inch guns fired projectiles weighing as much as 500 pounds at targets on Peddock's Island. In the 1890's the MDC took over the island and built a sewage treatment facility.

In 1950, the M.D.C. replaced this facility with a more modern primary sewage treatment plant. Nut Island will soon house the M.W.R.A. Southern Sewage Collection System Headworks. This new facility will filter hard matter from the inter-island tunnel. The old M.D.C. plant is scheduled for demolition in 1995.

A public park will be created on the island during the summer of 1996. Visitors will appreciate spectacular bay views from the walking and biking trails.

How to Get There: By auto—Off Route 3A at 147 Sea Ave., Quincy.

DIGGING UP THE PAST

To the casual visitor, the Boston Harbor Islands provide an interesting excursion; to the archaeologist, however, they are a working laboratory for uncovering the past. In fact, although many of the archaeological sites on the islands have been destroyed over the centuries by human settlement and by erosion, experts consider the Boston Harbor Islands (along with the adjacent river basins) to be the single most important area for understanding the early history of this part of the New England coast.

Over the last 20 years, archaeologists from the University of Massachusetts at Boston and other institutions have investigated most of the islands. Their primary purpose has been to discover and inventory all remaining archaeological sites in order to protect them from further destruction in the face of increased public recreation. In a few cases, sites in immediate danger of destruction have been thoroughly excavated.

These studies are also the first step in reconstructing the pieces of a vast jigsaw puzzle: the culture of the Native Americans in the Boston Harbor area. Archaeologists have begun to learn about prehistoric economic systems and their long-term impact on the Harbor's environment—with the ultimate objective of better understanding our own impact on the marine and terrestrial environments.

There is scientific evidence that people first arrived in the vicinity of Boston Harbor about 10,000 years ago, after the glaciers that covered this area during the Ice Age had melted away. We know very little about the life of these first people, but we do know that by about 7000 years ago they were well settled into eastern Massachusetts, and that they lived by hunting, fishing, and gathering wild resources. Deer provided their most important source of meat; they also fished in the rivers and marshlands, and collected a wide variety of seeds, nuts, berries, fruits, and roots.

The distinctive tools of these early people have been found on several of the Islands. However, geologists believe that the sea level was much lower in these early times, and that the islands were hills in a marsh plain, rather than islands in a harbor. Most of the locations where tools have been found would have been next to rivers, and if they camped at all on the coast, those sites have been drowned. Long Island boasts the oldest artifact from a Harbor Island, a spearpoint about 9000 years old, and Peddocks has produced the oldest human skeletal remains, dated about 4100 years ago.

By about 3000 years ago, sea levels had risen enough so that the harbor islands became actual islands. In all probability, access to some of these islands (such as Grape and Thompsons) was considerably easier than today, but others (such as Long and Calf) could only be reached by dugout canoe. Nevertheless, the rich coastal environment made these trips worthwhile. As shellfish beds developed, people began to adapt to the marine environment along the coast, and their camps became numerous. Middens, large ancient garbage dumps of clamshells left by the Indians, have been found on a number of the islands, and these middens are rich in food remains. These suggest that Indians probably crossed over to these islands knowing the salt and freshwater marshes there provided a wide variety of easily obtainable food such as ducks and fish. Deer, as well as raccoon and other small mammals, also lived on many of the islands and were hunted by the Indians who camped there. Some of these animals fled the mainland to escape from wolves and other predators, either by crossing mudflats at low tide, swimming, or crossing the ice in winter. Before the modern era brought thermal pollution, the Harbor frequently froze over.

Fish bones and shells indicate that they caught cod and a variety of other fish, and that they collected clams and oysters. They also continued to eat plant foods, and may have begun to experiment with many kinds of weeds which have been overlooked by modern people as a source of nourishment. Perhaps further study of this period will unlock secrets of the ways these people managed their ecology—lessons that could be vital for a world in search of new food resources to feed itself.

Sometime after about A.D. 1000, corn, beans, and squash began to be used by coastal tribes. These crops were first domesticated far to the south in Mexico. They were traded to tribes in the Southwest and then into the Midwest, where Native American horticulturalists gradually developed varieties that could withstand the colder climate and shorter growing season of the Northeast. As they incorporated farming into their economy, there is evidence that the Indians on the Boston Harbor Islands changed the way the islands were used, clearing plots for gardens and perhaps incorporating entire islands into their defended territories. These changes make this late period intriguing to scientists interested in the relationship between humans and their environments. The Boston Harbor Islands undoubtedly hold many of the answers to our questions about this important topic.

Barbara Luedtke
Department of Anthropology
University of Massachusetts, Boston

HINGHAM HARBOR ISLANDS

There are four small islands in Hingham Harbor—Langlee, Ragged, Sarah and Button. All of them are owned by the Town of Hingham; all are bedrock outcroppings covered with underbrush and trees. The total area of the islands is only 10 acres, and except for a few small beaches, their shorelines are rockbound.

Ragged Island

Comprising nearly four acres, Ragged Island was the only island in Hingham Harbor to ever be inhabited. John Langlee bought several of the islands in the harbor in 1686 and settled with his family on Ragged.

One story has it that he named the island Ragged after his daughter, who was nicknamed Ragged Sarah, for her casual dress. (Note the names of two other islands: Sarah and Langlee.)

In the late nineteenth century, another owner built a footbridge connecting the island with the mainland where there was a summer resort. A restaurant and observation post, no longer standing, were built on the island in 1880. Today the island is still a popular summertime spot for picnickers and boaters.

Scene on Ragged Island.

Sarah Island

This two-acre island was owned by John Langlee at the same time he resided on Ragged Island. It is covered with a few stands of pine, larch, birch and small maples. The island's rocky shore makes it difficult to approach by boat.

Langlee Island

Approximately four acres in size, Langlee has two small sandy beaches, a variety of trees and an interesting geological formation called puddingstone—a pebble conglomerate of various shapes, sizes and colors mixed with gravel, which resembles a plum pudding. Langlee is a favorite picnic spot for boaters.

Button

The smallest island in Hingham Harbor, Button covers less than one acre. Its rocky shoreline makes it difficult to approach by boat.

How to Get There: All the islands in Hingham Harbor can be reached by boat, but access to Sarah and Button are difficult.

Hingham Harbor Islands

WORLD'S END

As our journey through the islands draws to a close, it is fitting that the last stop be South Shore peninsula known as World's End. As the visitor gazes out from the heights of this peninsula overlooking Hingham Bay, he can see the tidal marshes, the solitary flight of a seagull, the city skyline, the Harbor, the Atlantic—the entire experience of the Boston Harbor Islands unfolds beneath him.

While the topography of World's End, with its 248 acres of rolling fields, tree-lined drives and five miles of rugged shoreline, differs from that of the Harbor Islands, it shares their history. Like most of the islands, World's End is a drumlin formation: in this case, two smooth, egg-shaped hills composed of glacial till. Indians camped there in the summer. After the arrival of the white man, the land was farmed continuously for over three centuries, well into the twentieth century. In the latter part of the nineteenth century, World's End also became a summer resort for wealthy Bostonians.

In 1890, John Brewer, owner of World's End, hired Frederick Law Olmsted, the famed landscape architect who designed both Central Park in New York and the Boston park system, to draw up a park plan for his estate. Gravel paths, lined with oak, hickory and red cedar trees and following the contour of the land, were constructed, transforming World's End into a New England version of the Elysian fields. On the land was Brewer's huge wood-shingled mansion and a sprawling farm that included stables, barns, blacksmith shop, greenhouse, poultry house, workers' quarters and windmills. Prize Jersey cattle grazed on the rolling pasture land. On the hillsides grew fields of hay, corn, oats, sugar beets, alfalfa and vegetables.

Unfortunately, the Brewer family line died out in 1936. Eventually the cows were sold and the buildings were torn down. But trustees of the estate managed to protect the land against urban encroachment and the

World's End

construction of a nuclear power plant until 1967. At that time, with the threat of development growing, the Trustees of Reservations, a private Massachusetts conservation organization, stepped in to purchase the land to protect and preserve it for public enjoyment.

Today, World's End provides a spectrum of many of the microenvironments found on the islands themselves. There are rocky beaches, ledges and cliffs, patches of salt marsh and a freshwater marsh dominated by cattails and bulrushes. The grassy fields in various stages of growth offer a study in the evolution of vegetation, from young meadows to plants and shrubs and finally to stands of mature trees.

Along with nature's hand is that of man's. Manicured hedgerows border old fields. Groves and formal tree plantings of native and exotic species line the gravel paths in accordance with Olmsted's plan. This diverse landscape in turn provides shelter and food for a variety of wildlife including quail, pheasant, foxes, rabbits and numerous migratory seashore birds.

In this age when man has come to be viewed as a destructive force in nature, World's End is a small but glowing example of man as a constructive force capable of both preserving nature's beauty and improving upon his own environment.

Facilities: Trails for nature study, scenic viewing, cross-country skiing and snowshoeing. Fishing is permitted. Horseback riding by permit only. Contact Trustees of Reservations, S.E. Regional office, 183 Whiting Street #3, Hingham or telephone 749-5780. Limited parking available. Open seven days, 10:00 A.M. to sunset. Nature walks and other events, such as the gathering for the Summer Solstice, are periodically offered. Contact the office for a newsletter and calendar of events. The entrance fee is $3.50 per person. There is no fee for members.

How to Get There: Follow Route 3A South. Take a left on Summer Street in Hingham. Proceed to Martin's Lane.

Hingham Harbor from World's End

Tall Ships Parade, Bicentennial 1976

THE SHORT, HAPPY LIFE OF A CLAM

The shallow, muddy flats in Hingham Harbor, as well as those off several Boston Harbor Islands and the Harbor shoreline itself, are abundant clam grounds. Hingham Harbor's mudflats were formed with the help of Hull peninsula, which protected the harbor from the strong Atlantic ocean currents and enabled silt to accumulate, forming mudflats. Even before the white settlers arrived, the Indians dug for clams in these mudflats. And as the Indians discovered, the soft-shell variety found in these parts (also known today as steamers) is edible and tasty.

Clams spawn during the period from July to September in these waters. The larvae, juveniles and adults, feed on microscopic plankton which they filter from the water. After the larva metamorphoses into juvenile and then adult form, the clam settles to the bottom. A juvenile clam wanders about, using its muscular foot, or is carried by currents until it is nearly one inch long. Then the clam generally establishes a burrow in the bottom and digs deeper as it grows. An adult clam found in these waters measures anywhere from one to three inches long.

Clam diggers harvest the clams with hand hoes or forks on the mudflats at low tide. Because of pollution, only commercial clam-diggers are permitted to harvest clams in Hingham Harbor and Hingham Bay. The Massachusetts Department of Public Health has classified virtually all of the productive shellfish flats in the bay as restricted, requiring shellfish purification prior to human consumption.

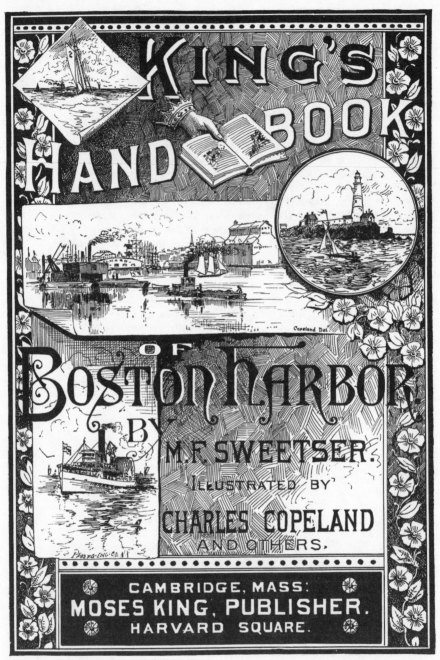

A centennial paperback edition of King's Handbook is available from the Friends of the Boston Harbor Islands.

DIRECTORY

LANDLUBBER TOURS

There are more than a few historic and scenic sights along the shores of Boston Harbor. All of them are accessible by auto. Here are some recommended points of interest.

Boston

Castle Island and Fort Independence—William J. Day Blvd., South Boston (see chapter on Castle Island).

Boston Fish Pier—mornings in the early part of the week is the best time to watch fish being unloaded. On Northern Ave., South Boston.

Boston Tea Party Ship and Museum—Danish-built replica of the *Beaver*, famous Tea Party brig. Moored at Fort Point Channel at the Congress St. bridge, off Atlantic Ave. near South Station. Open daily, 9-7. Among the museum's treasures is a "near authenticated" colonial tea chest.

New England Aquarium—Central Wharf at the foot of State St., off Atlantic Ave. Public transportation—MBTA, Aquarium station. Open weekdays, 9-5; weekends and holidays, 10-6.

Boston Waterfront Historic District—Includes Haymarket Square, Faneuil Hall, Quincy Market, Long, Commercial, and Lewis wharves, Located between New Congress St. and Atlantic Ave. Public transportation—MBTA, Haymarket or Aquarium station.

U.S.S. Constitution—"Old Ironsides," the renowned 44-gun frigate undefeated in forty battles, has recently been restored. Public transportation—MBTA City Square stop, Charlestown.

Forty Steps Beach, Nahant

North of Boston

Leaving Boston's waterfront, drive north through the Callahan Tunnel to East Boston. Logan International Airport as well as the docks of East Boston are good places to view Boston Harbor, particularly the Inner Harbor.

Continuing north on the East Boston Expressway, turn off on Rte. 145 (Bennington St.). Follow route (it becomes Saratoga St. and then Pleasant St.) to Winthrop. A public access site with parking and benches is located on Shirley St. and Deer Island Road. This is a good place to watch Logan Airport traffic. In the foreground is Snake Island, a lone survivor of Logan's expansion during the 1950's. Two other islands, Apple and Governor's (the latter once a beautiful 73-acre island occupied in early days by Puritan Governor John Winthrop), were both leveled and incorporated as part of the runway system.

For a coastal experience, drive north on Winthrop Parkway and then Revere Beach Blvd.; then to Rte. 1A through Lynn to Nahant. This peninsula town jutting out into the Atlantic is slightly beyond the scope of a description of Boston Harbor. But its winding roads, fishing coves, and Forty Steps Beach—rocky cliffs and ledges reminiscent of the Maine coast—are a delightful surprise. And Nahant's melange of suburban and summer homes, fishing shanties and Victorian mansions, offers a picture of a charming if eclectic seacoast community a short driving distance from Boston.

South of Boston

Driving south of Boston on Rte. 3 (the Southeast Expressway), you notice on your left in Dorchester Bay the colorful abstraction on a Boston Gas tank painted by a nun named Corita Kent a few years ago.

Turning off Rte. 3 at Exit 20 (Neponset-Quincy), pick up Quincy Shore Drive. Just before Wollaston Beach, turn left at E. Squantum St. (at the Shell Station). You are now in Squantum.

At this point, as the roadside sign notes, you are at Moswetuset Hummock, the seat of Chikatawbut, a chief of the Moswetusets. (It was from this Indian tribe, by the way, that the state of Massachusetts derived its name.) From the hummock, which is across the street from the Myles Standish elementary school, a little woodsy path leads up the hill to a point overlooking the islands of Quincy Bay.

Continuing along E. Squantum St., bear left following the seawall onto Dorchester St. (the same street that leads to Long Island). On this stretch of the road are good views of Dorchester Bay, the Boston campus of the University of Massachusetts, and the Boston skyline. As you drive up a hill, just before the building on your left marked South Shore Rehabilitation Center, you will come upon a natural 17-acre shoreline park called Squaw Rock.

The park, which is an expansive knoll with rocky ridges and rolling meadows cradled in between, is bounded by water on three sides and commands a view of the Boston skyline, Thompson Island directly offshore (you can see Thompson meadow and woodland), and the Harbor. It is a pleasant walk to the DAR monument erected in 1855 to Captain Myles Standish and Squanto, his Indian guide, who landed at this site in 1621.

According to one legend, Squaw Rock was named after an Indian woman who fell from it into the sea. The legend extends to the Squantum peninsula. The area was called Squaw Tumble or "Squan-tum." More likely though, the name Squaw Rock can be accounted for by the fact that the rock resembles an Indian profile. And Squantum took its name from Squanto, the Indian who not only accompanied Myles Standish on his explorations, but is credited with introducing the Pilgrims to corn, that essential food that helped keep them alive during their first trying year at Plymouth colony.

Continuing on the road past the Rehabilitation Center, you come first to Moon Island and then to Long Island (see chapters on these islands). Turning around, retrace your steps to Quincy Shore Drive, turn left and drive past Wollaston Beach for another good view of Quincy Bay. Turn left after tidal flats following Quincy Shore Drive or four blocks afterward on Sea St. Either road takes you out to Houghs Neck. This peninsula is a coastal community replete with coves, inlets, boatyards, fishermen's cottages, and a hill commanding views of both Quincy and Hingham bays. Nut Island is part of the peninsula and Raccoon Island is right offshore.

Returning to Rte. 3A, drive south to Hingham Harbor. At the rotary, take Summer St. and turn left at Martin's Lane for World's End, one of the most beautiful spots in Boston Harbor, or for that matter, all of New England (see chapter on World's End). Returning to Summer St., turn left and follow the road to Washington Blvd. This road leads to Nantasket Beach and Hull.

The town of Hull is a long peninsula that encloses Hingham Bay and Harbor from the Atlantic Ocean. Once known as Nantascot, a fishing station dating back to 1622, the area was settled by Puritans in 1630 and later named Hull. A tour of Hull offers a number of recreational and scenic pleasures. Perhaps the best known

Squaw Rock with University of Massachusetts' Boston Campus in Background

of these was Paragon Park, a classic amusement area, which was sold to make room for condominiums. The famous carousel remains. Nantasket Beach is an excellent bathing beach.

Off of Nantasket Ave., the town's central artery, you can tour such areas as Sunset Point, a charming little peninsula of beach homes, overlooking World's End, the Hingham Harbor Islands, the Weir River, Bumpkin Island and the hook of Hull. Continuing along the bay side of Hull, you will have good views of Quincy Bay and Bumpkin Island in the foreground, then Slate, Grape, Peddock's and the little outcroppings of Sheep Island in the background. Again, there is the Boston skyline faintly in the distance—a constant reminder that even amidst these lovely seascapes, you are never far from an urban center. On this side of Hull is also A Street Pier, where boats and fishing tackle can be rented.

Following Nantasket Ave., drive uphill after the alphabet-lettered streets to Point Allerton. From this hill you will have excellent views of the Atlantic Ocean and the rocky, sea-buffeted Brewsters and Boston Light. The Victorian architecture —featuring fanciful turrets and gables—is also interesting. Close offshore on the bay side, connected by a causeway, is Hog Island—formerly an Air Force radar station, now declared U.S. Government surplus property.

Last stop in Hull is Pemberton Point, the tip of the peninsula. Hull High School is located here, as well as boat and fishing tackle rentals. Looming directly across the channel (known as Hull Gut) are the eastern slopes of Peddock's Island, and you can easily distinguish the island's little wooden New England church and Fort Andrews. Farther out in the bay you can see Rainsford, George's, Lovell's, Moon and Long islands.

You can also reach Hull by ferryboat. Bay State Cruise Company operates a commuter ferry from Long Wharf in Boston to Pemberton Point. (For information on schedules and fares, call 723-7800.)

Hull in Days Gone By

THE HOTEL PEMBERTON, AT WINDMILL POINT, HULL.

TIPS ON VISITING THE ISLANDS

Weather is very unpredictable on the Harbor and there are few sheltered areas. Dress appropriately according to pre-departure weather information, which can be obtained from the National Weather Bureau (Tel: 569-3700) or use the following radio bands: 2450 or 2566 kilohertz, which carry weather information at 10:20 and 11:20 A.M. or 10:20 P.M. Continuous weather information is also available on F.M. at 162.55 megahertz.

Pit toilets (no running water) are available on many islands. Potable water is not available on many islands. Bring your own drinking water. (See *Facilities* of specific islands.)

Take along a first aid kit and treat cuts or abrasions promptly. This is especially important on islands frequented by seagulls, since their droppings contain bacteria which may produce infection.

Be sure to secure your boat on shore from tidal fluctuations, sudden squalls, theft and vandalism.

Protect your personal belongings from theft and vandalism.

These are your islands. Keep them clean. Please carry off all trash and litter.

Island ecology is very fragile. Be careful not to cut or destroy any trees or other island flora.

For 24-hour Coast Guard Rescue Service telephone 565-9200 or call the Boston Marine Radio Operator on Channel 16 F.M. and ask for Point Allerton or Port Security Station, Boston.

Open fires are not permitted on any of the islands, and firewood is not available. Bring your own charcoal or wood, and grills or stoves for cooking. All fires must be on the beach, below the high-tide line. Be sure to extinguish your fire properly after use. Should a fire get out of control, alert the island manager.

At present, all clam flats in the Harbor are classified by the Division of Marine Fisheries as contaminated.

Poison ivy is very abundant on the islands. For your protection stay on cleared trails and group areas.

To identify poison ivy look for
3 leaflets, smooth and shiny on
both sides.
Leaflets may be irregulary toothed.

Poison Ivy

Poison sumac can be distinguished from sumac by the following: poison sumac pods are white. Sumac pods are red. Wings on stems of poison sumac are shiny. Sumac wings are furry.

BOSTON HARBOR ISLANDS STATE PARK INFORMATION

Since the early 1970's, the Boston Harbor Islands State Park has been managed by the Metropolitan District Commission (M.D.C.) and the Department of Environmental Management (D.E.M.) under the Executive Office of Environmental Affairs. Thompson Island is the only privately owned island, although it is part of the Park. Call or write to the agencies listed below for park information, overnight camping, group day use permits, and information regarding special events. No alcohol is permitted on the Harbor Islands.

M.D.C. Harbor Region: 98 Taylor Street, Dorchester, MA 02122. Telephone: 727-5290 for George's, Lovell's, Peddock's and Castle Islands.

D.E.M. Boston Harbor Islands State Park: 349 Lincoln Street, Building 45, Hingham, MA 02043. Telephone: 740-1605 for Gallop's, Grape, Bumpkin, Calf and all the Brewster Islands.

Thompson Island/Outward Bound Education Center: P.O. Box 127, South Boston, MA 02127. Telephone: 328-3900.

Resident island managers provide seasonal program services on the islands in the state park system. The Friends of the Boston Harbor Islands assist the staff through their on-island volunteer program. Contact the Friends at 523-8386 for information on membership, the on-island volunteer program and activities. The Friends sponsor boat trips to the islands all year long and in the evenings during the summer months.

All piers on the islands are subject to storm damage. Check with Park Headquarters before planning your first excursion to an island.

Bay State Cruise Company provides seasonal boat service to Georges Island from Long Wharf in Boston and the Hingham Shipyard. Call their office for information on inter-island trips (723-7800).

HARBOR CRUISES AND EXCURSIONS

A.C. Cruise Line, Northern Avenue, E. Boston. Telephone: 426-8419
Bay State Cruise Company, 67 Long Wharf, Boston. Telephone: 723-7800
Boston By Sail (Inner Harbor & Island tours aboard new 61' schooner) Long Wharf, Boston. Telephone: 742-3313
Boston Harbor Cruises, 63 Long Wharf, Boston. Telephone: 227-4320
Boston Harbor Whale Watch, Rowe's Wharf, Boston. Telephone: 345-9866
Massachusetts Bay Lines, 60 Rowe's Wharf, Boston. Telephone: 542-8000
N.E. Aquarium Whale Watch, Central Wharf, Boston. Telephone: 973-5277

CHARTER, FISHING AND PARTY BOATS

Boston Area

A.C. Cruise Line, Northern Avenue, 426-8419. Daily excursions to Gloucester, whale-watching, harbor and dinner cruises.

Boston Harbor Sailing Club, 72 East India Row, 523-2619. Cruising Sailboats 24'-39'.

Bay State Cruise Company, 20 Long Wharf, 723-7800. Daily harbor tours, service to Georges, Peddocks, and Nantasket Beach, sunset and dinner cruises, all-day excursions to Provincetown, Cape Cod, and the Islands.

Boston By Sail, 65 Lewis Wharf, 742-3313. Harbor cruises, island cruises, moonlight cruises. New addition to fleet: 61' schooner "Spirit." Many boats available for private charter.

Boston Harbor Cruises, 1 Long Wharf, 227-4320. Daily harbor tours and charters.

Captain Lou, 68 Edward Street, Medford, 396-4096. 48' fishing vessel "Sea King" departs from 246 Border Street, East Boston.

Charters Unlimited, Marina Bay, Quincy, 328-9224. Private boats for charter.

Majestic Charters, 50 Rowe's Wharf, 951-2460.

Massachusetts Bay Lines, Rowe's Wharf, 542-8000. Daily harbor island tours, dinner cruises, sunset cruises.

Midnight Charter, 35 Spring Street, Weymouth, 335-3298. Inshore, offshore fishing or private charter aboard two vessels, 34' Sport Fishing boat or 38' Novi.

Sail Boston Charters, 147-1 Cushing Street, Cambridge, 354-1131. Boats of various sizes and types available for private charter.

Spirit of Boston Charters, 256 Marginal Street, 569-4449. Clambake, luncheon and dinner cruises, harbor island cruises.

Spirit of Massachusetts, Bldg. 1, Charlestown Navy Yard, 242-1414. 125' gaff-rigged schooner available for private charter and educational programming.

Swift Yacht Charters, 26 Summer Street, Hingham, 749-8340. Various sizes and types of sailboats available for private charter.

Embarking on a Harbor Cruise

PIERS AND BOAT LAUNCHING SITES
(P=Pier, L=Launch Site)

Boston
Charlestown Navy Yard, Pier 4   (P)
Malibu Beach, Morrissey Blvd.   (L)
Commercial Point, Morrissey Blvd.   (L)
Castle Island   (P)
Orient Heights Beach, East Boston   (L)
40 New Street, East Boston   (L)
Kelly's Landing, South Boston   (P)
Little Mystic Channel, Charlestown—on Terminal St. near Bunker Hill and *U.S.S. Constitution*   (L)
Charles River, Msgr. William J. Daly Recreational Center, Nanantum Rd., Brighton-Newton   (L)

Boston Harbor
Bumpkin Island   (P)
Calf Island   (P)
Gallop's Island   (P)
George's Island   (P)
Grape Island   (P)
Great Brewster Island   (P)
Lovell's Island   (P)
Peddock's Island   (P)

Hingham
Hewitts Cove Marina   (L)
Iron Horse Statue Area   (L)

Hull
"A" Street Marine   (P) (L)
Gould's Boat Shop, Nantasket Pier   (L)
Pemberton Point   (P) (L)

Lynn
General Edward Bridge, Rte, 1A   (P)
Lynn Harbor Marine, Blossom Street   (L)
M.D.C. Playground   (L)
Mercury Outboard Center, Saugus Road   (L)

Marshfield
Green Harbor Marine   (L)
Humarock Marine   (L)
Mary's Livery   (L)
Town Pier (Green Harbor)   (L)

Nahant
Nahant Beach, Harbor Side   (L)

Quincy
Anchor Marine, 666 So. Artery   (L)
Bay's Water Marine   (L)
Hurley's Boat Rental   (P) (L)
Marina Bay, Squantum   (L)

Revere
Holt's Pier   (P)
Simpson's Pier   (P)

Saugus
Fishermen's Outlet   (L)

Weymouth
Wessagusset, George E. Lane Beach
Neck Street   (L)
Tern Harbor Marina, River Street   (L)

Winthrop
Crystal Cove Marina, Shirley Street   (L)

Off Nantasket

SURF AND BELL BOAT, HARDING'S LEDGE, BOSTON HARBOR.

RENTAL ROWBOATS, MOTORBOATS AND SAILBOATS

Boston

Boston By Sail, 65 Lewis Wharf 742-3313. Sailboats and motorboats.
Boston Harbor Sailing Club, 72a E. India Row, 523-2619. Sailboats by membership only.
Boston Sailing Center, 54 Lewis Wharf, 227-4198. Sailboats by membership only.

Hull

Pemberton Marine, 173 Main Street, 925-0239. Skiffs w/outboard motors.

Marshfield

Mary's Boat Livery, 2205 Rte. 3A, 837-2322.

Quincy

Hurley's Boat Rental, 136 Bay View Avenue, Hough's Neck, 479-1239. Skiffs w/outboard motors.

Salem

Salem Willows Boat Livery, Salem Willows Park, 745-6996. Rowboats.

Commuter Boats to Boston

Boston Harbor Commuter Services, 740-1253. Offers weekday service between the Hingham Shipyard and Rowes Wharf in Boston. Also runs a daily airport shuttle from Rowes Wharf.
Boston Harbor Cruises, 227-4321. Offers seven day service between Long Wharf in Boston and the Charlestown Navy Yard.
Bay State Cruise Co., 723-7800. Offers weekday service between Pemberton Pier in Hull and Long Wharf in Boston.
Mass. Bay Lines, 542-8000. Offers weekday service between the Hingham Shipyard and Rowes Wharf in Boston.

HOW, WHERE, WHEN AND WHAT TO CATCH

Fishing is good off any wharf, pier, or jetty in Boston Harbor, except in the Inner Harbor where pollution makes it undesirable. Best fishing is from a boat or where the deep water comes near shore. Among a few top spots: the pier at Castle Island and City Point in South Boston; Commercial Point near the Boston Gas tanks in Dorchester; off the Columbia Point campus of U. Mass; Moon Island and Black's Creek (surf casting) along Quincy Shore Drive in Quincy; Weymouth Back River; in Hull Gut near Point Allerton.

Species	Season	Baits and Lures	Methods and Tackle
Striped Bass Min. length 33″	May through October	Sea worms, eels, squid, "Pogies," mackerel, jigs, plugs, spinners	Casting with light to heavy tackle from shore or boat
Pollock	May through October	Almost any bait, jigs, spoons, feathers, plugs	Still fishing; casting from boat or shore; trolling
Mackerel	April through September	X-mas tree rig w/jig, clam bits, sea worms, squid strips	Light tackle; trolling; casting from shore or boat
Tautog Min. length 12″	May & June	Sea worms, crabs, sheelfish	Still fishing from boat or shore
Winter Flounder Min. length 12″	Year-round	Sea worms, squid strips, clam necks	Still fishing from boat, pier, breakwater
Cod Min. 17″	Year-round	Clams, sea worms, chubs, jigs	Still fishing from boat; casting from shore
Bluefish	May through October	"Pogies," mackerel, plugs, spinners	Casting from boat or shore; trolling
Smelt	Late Fall and Winter	Sea worms, grass shrimp, small jigs	Still fishing from boat or pier*

* Best spot is Hewitts Cove Marina, Hingham
SOURCE: Massachusetts Division of Marine Fisheries

BAIT AND TACKLE

Boston
Broadway Bait and Tackle, 661-A E. Broadway, South Boston, 268-5674
Fishing Plus, 6 Redfield Street, Dorchester, 436-9231
P & J Bait Shop, 1397 Dorchester Avenue, Dorchester, 288-7917
Stoddard's, 50 Temple Place, Boston, 426-4187
Bob Smith's Sporting Goods, 6 Spring Lane, Boston, 426-4440

Danvers
Danversport Marine Center, 10 Harbor Street, 777-4400
Fishermen's Outfitters, Rte. 1 North, Box 238, 774-3958
MVP Sports, 107 High Street, 774-7512

Dedham
Tropicland, Inc., 100 Bridge Street, Rte. 109, 329-3777

Hingham
Landfall Marine Center, 433 Lincoln Street, Rte. 3A, 749-1255

Hull
Pemberton Marine, Inc., 173 Main Street, 925-0239

Quincy
Anchor Marine, 666 Southern Artery, 472-9507
Bayswater Marine, 15 Bayswater Road, 471-8060
Fore River Bait and Tackle, 708 Washington Street, 770-1397
Hurley's Boat Rental, Inc., 136 Bayview Avenue, 479-1239

Salem
Old Timers' Bait and Tackle, 6 Planters Street, 744-5742
Pete's Bait and Tackle, 121 North Street, 744-2262
Salem Willows Boat Livery, Salem Willows Park, 745-6996

Scituate
Trask Tackle, 787 Country Way, P.O. 248, 545-4228

SWIMMING BEACHES AROUND THE HARBOR

Boston
Malibu Beach—Morrissey Blvd., Dorchester
Savin Hill Beach—Morrissey Blvd., Dorchester
Tenean Beach—Morrissey Blvd., Dorchester
Constitution Beach—Orient Heights, East Boston
Carson Beach—Day Blvd., South Boston
Castle Island—Day Blvd., South Boston
City Point—Day Blvd., South Boston
M Street Beach—Day Blvd., South Boston
Pleasure Bay—Day Blvd., South Boston

Hull
Nantasket Beach—Rtes. 3, 3A, 128

Lynn
Kings Beach—Lynn Shore Drive
Lynn Beach—Lynn Shore Drive

Nahant
Nahant Beach—Nahant Rd.

Quincy
Wollaston Beach—Quincy Shore Drive

Revere
Revere Beach—Revere Beach Parkway
Short Beach—Winthrop Parkway

Winthrop
Winthrop Shore Drive

Nantasket Beach

PICTURE CREDITS

*Illustrations by Charles Copeland and others for M.F. Sweetser, *King's Handbook of Boston Harbor* (Cambridge, Mass., 1885).

INDEX